# it's happening

### a portrait of the youth scene today

# *it's* **happening**

**a portrait of the youth scene today**
*j. l. simmons and barry winograd*

M/L
*marc-laird publications*
*santa barbara, california*

## acknowledgments

nola simmons for suggesting the seminal thought of growing your own tree, for typing the manuscript, and for fixing
the tea during long hours of work. sam and teddi winograd
for assistance and encouragement in ways too numerous to
detail. les berry and ben logan for just being. and to the
others (necessarily unnamed) who contributed to this work.

# contents

***it's happening***

*a portrait of the youth scene today*

# 1 / where it's at

During noon hour the Berkeley campus plaza becomes a midway of happenings. You are confronted with a seemingly endless melange of display tables and impassioned speeches and strolling conversations, and almost all of the free space seems to be flooded with a sea of moving people, nameless people scurrying toward their private destinations. A small army of youths seated at the rows of tables are handing out pamphlets and seeking donations for racial equality, free speech, overseas children, the legalization of marijuana, saving the giant redwoods and the stunted Redman, sexual emancipation, slum relief, civil liberties defense funds, Vietnam orphans and Viet Cong blood. Sometimes the youths are waved to by friends; sometimes they are questioned by tourists; sometimes they are heckled by those who are operating under different flags.

As you stroll along, a young speaker shouts, "What are we doing in Vietnam?" Only a few paces away, another orator is decrying the mass production sham of the giant modern university, "How long since you've actually *seen* one of your professors?" Across the way a Negro leader raises his voice in competition, "You think we got integration in this land now, baby? You just go down to Watts; you just take a little ride through Alabama and see the nigger pickaninnies . . . . . ." A university band marches through and its precision brass temporarily drowns out both their voices and disturbs the pensive youngster staring out from under the shade of a newly planted sapling. A little further along the walk a well-dressed girl who looks like she could be your baby sitter next door, is speaking: "In our state most married couples would be legally subject to long jail sentences for the lovemaking they practice in the privacy of their own bedrooms. Your doctor or minister is legally party to a felony just for handing out any of the standard marriage manuals. How long will these hypocrisies go on?"

But you soon realize that tables and speakers are only landmarks in a welter of overlapping and ongoing scenes. There comes over you the feeling of a bustle in the air and this feeling grows into a realization that a thousand and one happenings are occurring all around you. Over near the fountain, a bearded youth is gazing into the cascading drops of water. He looks up and says to nobody in particular, "How can we do it, how? But it's to be done." A short distance away you see one student giving another his paperback copy of Aldous Huxley's *Island* and telling him earnestly that it's really a trip. Over against the stone column of a building a girl is crying quietly. And by the entrance to the Student Union's outdoor terrace, two men are exchanging a ten dollar bill for an envelope with two 500 microgram capsules of LSD inside. "This is full potency Sandoz so be cool," the dealer cautions before moving on. As you step around a kissing couple, disjointed bits of passing conversations reach your ears.

"Have you heard Donavan's new . . . "

"I don't know if I can."

"Schumann's missed the whole point of China's . . . "

"He's copped out . . . "

"Cool it, here comes . . . "

"Hey, man, what's happening?"

"Well, anybody might think of suicide after . . . "

2

" . . . who ya kiddin', twenty bucks for a lid of that shit!"

"They said they wouldn't give me a job unless . . . "

"I doubt it, I really doubt it."

" . . . well then, screw Johnson."

"You're never gonna make it."

" . . . I hope . . . "

The seasoned inhabitants are ignoring most of the happenings around them and are pursuing their own private lives. But a well attired middle-aged couple, walking arm-in-arm, a Kodak camera clutched in the wife's left hand, are gazing about them with the wide-eyed incredulity of innocents abroad. They seem almost to huddle together against that something in the wind that is what's happening and the man keeps shaking his head. "It sure wasn't anything like this when we were going, was it. I don't like the Republicans, but, maybe Reagan's right about clamping down on the colleges. Hate to put harnesses on anybody. But can we let Janice come here?" The woman smiles toward the CORE booth but frowns at a girl's sweater with a button that reads, "Make love, not war." The man smiles tolerantly at the still kissing couple but his mind is troubled again by his little girl's enrollment here. The persisting rumors of widespread marijuana smoking in her high school; going off all the time for some reason or other with kids he hadn't even met; the growing piles of phonograph records that seemed awfully frank about an awful lot of things; the way she sometimes looked at him when he tried to talk to her. He had the queasy realization these days that he no longer knew what she was thinking or doing or getting herself into when she was away from the house. Maybe nothing, maybe everything.

As the man and woman look at the swirl of scenes around them, they both are only beginning to catch a first glimmering of awareness that this is a showcase of what is happening throughout our society and in some form or other, among virtually all segments of our populace—an undiluted and vanguard cameo of a social revolution in which we are all direct or indirect participants and which holds fair promise of transforming the American Way of Life. As Janice's parents leave the main plaza (which only two years ago was jammed with ten thousand supporters of the now famous Berkeley Free Speech Movement) and cross over to walk by the shops and cafes down Telegraph Avenue (which only a year ago was jammed with twenty thousand Vietnam peace marchers) they are walking along the surface of a world that is mysterious and subterranean to their own, a world which will remain mostly closed to them forever, unless they somehow learn to cross the chasm of divergent views which separate them from it.

Anyone walking along the Avenue immediately south of this sprawling State property, knows he's where it's at. "It's a carnival, man. Things have really turned on up here," a long-time Berkeley and San Francisco veteran remarks on the change the Bay Area has undergone in the last couple years. There is no real separation, in the happening world, between campus and off-campus, between the Bay Area and the entire West Coast scene, between the West Coast and the rest of the country, or even so much between America and the rest of the world. Such boundaries are set up and cherished by officials and Establishments, but the happeners are highly mobile both in body and in mind, and particular places are important only as possible locales of happenings and convenient ports of call.

The action you see in the main plaza and down the Avenue and across the bridge in the Haight-Ashbury district is a many-faced but unified theme that is now being re-enacted with variations in other cities, and even small towns across the country. It is only a part, however, of the total American landscape, a small part which doesn't reflect the quiet conforming Americanism of the majority of students and youths in even the most swinging locales. What's happening is still a minority group phenomenon and only a small fraction of our nation's populace is directly involved in the adventures and misadventures of these emerging life-styles. But these actions gain new converts each day, despite a good deal of disapproval and harassment from the more conventional sectors of our society. And these happenings, unlike most earlier developments on the edges of our society, are confronting and challenging—and thus involving—the rest of the nation.

But, there is no simple answer to the question "What's happening?" The variety of things now occurring in America seem so bewildering at first glance that the observer is tempted to conclude that everyone has gone a little bit mad. Has America (and much of the rest of the world, it seems) been caught up in a collective fever like the dancing craze of the Middle Ages or lemmings rushing headlong into the sea? Have we come to a time of decadent debauchery as in the latter days of the Roman Empire? Or are we in the midst of a process of breakthrough into a brave new world where living will be richer and fuller for everyone?

Those involved in making the happenings are, in a sense, innocents abroad too—explorers and first settlers in the largely unmapped wilderness of the raw immediate present. While last generation's scholars and artists and officials are struggling to understand and deal with the contemporary world, the swingers are simply running out into it. To many older people this heedless plunge into untried waters seems hasty and foolhardy; a horde of modern Don Quixotes drenched in their own delusions, tilting with windmills which may come round to knock them down, and set upon a pilgrimage to nowhere. Sure, there are difficult times and we've got problems, but let's try and be sensible and proper.

Yet today is the draft notice and the girl who talks with you about the taste of honey. Today is the problem of growing up absurd and of parents out of tune. Today is the teacher mumbling in a dead language and deciding on your right to be in on the Great Society Game. Today is blowing in the wind.

## 2 / the hang-loose ethic

The happenings described in the last chapter are the concrete manifestations of an emerging new ethos in American society, which seems most aptly called "the hang-loose ethic." It is cool and irreverent and it reflects a good deal of disaffection toward many of our more traditional roots. For this reason, it is perhaps more worrisome to parents, educators, and officials than the mere wildness or deviant flirtations of youth.

A barefooted man with a beard and a surplus Navy jacket that had "Love IS" written on the back of it was walking down the main street of a small midwestern city, digging the sunlight and thinking that the heat was really pleasant when you got out into it. A group of high school kids rode by him in a car and began shouting to him. "Hey beatnik." "Hey, you're high man." "What color's your dingy?" And, from one of the less imaginative boys, "Why don't you go fly a kite?"

The man looked up musingly, jaywalked across the street to a dime store, bought a kite and some luminous paint and two thousand feet of string. He took them to his battered car and drove around the adjacent suburbs for awhile, rounding up kids to fly the kite with him. Some parents looked him over and scurried their kids away, shaking their heads about the invasion of perverts; others looked into his face and saw nothing evil there, so consented. They drove to the top of a hill overlooking the town, painted the kite with bright psychedelic colors, sent it up and flew it all afternoon. Toward sunset, they cut loose the string and watched their *objet d'art* disappear into the aerial world above them.

The thing about this story is that the young man didn't turn upon his assailants and by opposing them become their likes. Nor did he go into a foetal crouch over a beer, pitying himself as a sensitive and misunderstood soul (which he is) and condemning the society which trains even its children to put down the unusual. He transcended the harassment, rather than succumbing to it by being roused to self-pity or anger.

The emerging ethic is hang-loose in a number of senses, but, its deep-running feature is that things once taken for granted as God-given or American Constitution-given—those basic premises about the world and the way it works —are no longer taken for granted or given automatic allegiance. In other words, many Americans are hanging a bit loose from traditional Americana.

This new ethos is still in the process of forming and emerging; the adherents themselves are mostly unaware of the credo they are participating in making and are already living by. For instance, if you went up to many of the likely young people about town and said, "Say, are you an adherent of the hang-loose ethic?", many of them would look at you oddly and wonder what the hell you were talking about.

Well, if this thing is still so amorphous and you can only speculate about it, and the supposed followers are hardly even aware of it, why bother?

Because we want to see what lies beneath the legion of different concrete happenings. A society can be portrayed in a number of different ways and each gives a different picture of what the society is. It can be done by sketching the material objects, the streets, the buildings, the childhood and adult toys. It can be done by describing the typical behavior, the activities, the rituals, the average life-course of an ordinary member. It can also be done by trying to ferret out the underlying ideology or ethos, which comes forth in a thousand and one different ways and which is the wellspring from which flows the other things, the toys, the scenes, the lives, the typical attitudes and responses. Our attempt to ferret out the ideology behind the happenings is an attempt, then, to dive beneath the trappings and veneers down to the basic world view of the people who are making them happen.

At first glance, it might seem as if the hang-loose ethic is the absence of any morality, that it rejects every ideology, that the followers have no rudder and no star except the swift gratification of all impulses. At a second glance it appears only as a bewildering melange of scenes in various locales. But upon closer examination, one can see that it does embody some values and some guiding principles which, although still ill-formed and vaguely expressed, shape the attitudes and actions of the followers. However, to convey a fuller picture of this ethos, we must sketch the previous American ethics from which it emerged.

Europeans and Americans of the past few centuries have been characterized by most writers as human beings who subscribed to and lived by what is called the Protestant Ethic. This Protestant Ethic was a way of life and a view of life which stressed the more somber virtues, like the quiet good feeling of a hard day's work well done, the idea that the good man always more than earned his pay, and a kind of fierce pragmatism in which the hard and fast, here and now, seeable, touchable, aspects of reality were the only things given the name of reality.

Another thing about the Protestant Ethic was a kind of

positive moderatism. Moderation wasn't just a safe course between extremes; moderation was an optimum, positive, good in-and-of-itself thing. Moderation was raised almost to a first principle of ethics. It was a mandate on how to conduct your life.

Anything which veered very far from this somber dignity in oneself and one's accumulations was thought of as bad and suspect. We will see, for example, when we discuss "tripping" that whereas most of the world has regarded exceptional behavior that strays beyond the mundane with an awe combining wonder and terror, in the Western world the wonder has until very recently dropped away and it was suppressed as altogether dangerous. Western man neglected what other times and places made a good deal of, the positive aspects which exceptional experiences might have.

This moderatism carried over into virtually every aspect of the lives of the people. Even in religion and young love, anything smacking too much of mysticism was suspect. The West has relied mostly upon dogma rather than experience in its religious institutions and, despite our hungry romanticism, most of our marriages and other sexual liasons have been made largely by arrangement.

This Protestant Ethic seems to have characterized the majority of our forefathers although there was always a "lunatic" fringe and a subterranean stratum composed of those at the bottom of the social ladder and of outsiders. And, like all people everywhere, the adherents didn't entirely live up to their own ideals. But, the Protestants ran the schools and the courts and the country and the fringe was contained and circumscribed, largely kept at the fringe.

Then, as the decades passed and we moved into the present century, America began to undergo a secularization which involved not only a dwindling of the force of religion but also a dwindling of the force of the work ethic and the rather stiff personal code which surrounded it. Particularly in the mushrooming urban areas after the Second World

War, something grew up which William F. Whyte termed "the Social Ethic."

The Social Ethic (or perhaps more aptly, the Sociable Ethic) was a kind of jocular, benign, superficial, "we're all in the same boat," goodwill. But it shared many things with the Protestant Ethic from which it evolved under the impact of modern times. It was still taken for granted that getting ahead in the Establishment was the thing to do, and that the accumulation of material wealth was a good thing in and of itself. Whyte used the "organization man" living in the new suburbs as his prototypic example and he made a good argument that this was tending to become the overweening American ethos. Work and play, family and politics, each of these were supposed to be a good thing, a fun thing, a comfortable thing. The Sociable Ethic was a secularization of the Protestant ideology combined with a feeling of comfort and goodwill which is easy to generate in a luxuriant society such as ours.

Risk is minimized in the Sociable Ethic. All parties join in a collusion which reduces the chance of great failure and great success once you've been hooked into the system. Of course, there were some dark counterthemes in this portrait: those thirty percent of the people who were not in any real sense beneficiaries of the luxuriant system. And it certainly was not a comfortable place for them—it was as Baldwin has suggested, another country. This didn't just mean the Negro of the South; it also included most Northern Negroes, the uneducated, the abysmally poor, those who lacked the skills to sell themselves, to make themselves an attractive enough package to get recruited into the system.

But the majority of Americans were in it and were doing fairly well. And the continuities with the earlier ethic remained. There still existed a kind of blandness, a real distrust for the exceptional and the bizarre, and there still remained a real distrust for doing something, let's say, "just for kicks." We had in the fifties almost the Utopian culmination of the principle of moderation. Moderate in politics, moderate in work—not too much because it doesn't really pay, not too little because you might get dropped. Moderate in family which involved a kind of thing where you were moderately attached to your spouse and children and moderately concerned with their welfare and you were moderately unfaithful and moderately blasphemous. But you also gave a moderate allegiance to your family and your company and your country.

This was not a picture window nightmare. Most of those involved were probably moderately comfortable and moderately happy.

Does this mean that these people were apathetic and uninvolved, just going through some motions?

No. They were moderately involved in many things. They cried a little and they cared a little and they strove a little and were proud a little and ashamed a little. You see, these people were veterans of hard times; a world depression which was tough, a world war which was tough, an uncertain time afterwards which was tough. And so at last they arrived in their ranch houses and they could afford cocktails on the way home without much worrying about the price. It was, in a sense, the indulgence of a dream, the dream of building an affluent society. Because in the fifties that's exactly what we had—fantastically affluent compared with anything that had ever existed before.

Certainly, there were a few hot social movements and protests about the thirty percent who weren't "in." But, we must realize that in most times and countries it's been 90% or 98%. So only thirty percent left out is pretty damn good and something brand new in history. And the first scattered appearance of the beats and the freedom cats must not obscure the fact that the vast majority were (moderately) good Americans in the small sense of not rocking any boats.

Yet even as the sociable ideology was crystallizing and

taking hold and Eisenhower was virtually proclaiming moderation the cornerstone of our national policy, a new kind of feeling was beginning to stir across the land—a feeling which had many ties with the past but which was also new.

Although there were precursors in the late fifties when Ginsberg was telling people he'd seen the best minds of his generation driven mad, and hip talk (and an inevitable bit of the philosophy behind it) was being picked up by teenagers, the hang-loose ethos really belongs to the sixties because this is the decade in which it is emerging and spreading throughout our society.

When we search for the "philosophy" which is the common denominator running through the variety of happenings—the implicit code of values pushing those involved toward some things and away from other things—some of the characteristics of this yet crystallizing view can be discerned.

One of the fundamental characteristics of the hang-loose ethic is that it is *irreverent*. It repudiates, or at least questions, such cornerstones of conventional society as Christianity, "my country right or wrong," the sanctity of marriage and premarital chastity, civil obedience, the accumulation of wealth, the right and even competence of parents, the schools, and the government to head and make decisions for everyone—in sum, the Establishment. This irreverence is probably what most arouses the ire and condemnation of the populace. Not only are the mainstream institutions and values violated, but their very legitimacy is challenged and this has heaped insult upon moral injury in the eyes of the rank and file.

Sin, as the violation of sacred beliefs and practices, is nothing new and most of us have had at least a few shamefully delightful adventures somewhere along the way. But what is qualitatively new is that the very truth and moral validity of so many notions and practices, long cherished in our country, are being challenged. When caught by parents or authorities, youths are no longer hanging their heads in shame. Instead, they are asserting the rightness, at least for themselves, of what they're doing. And they are asking what right do their elders have to put them down?

And not infrequently the irreverence takes a form which goes beyond this openly aggressive challenging. An increasing number of happeners have reached a level of disrespect so thoroughgoing that they don't even bother to "push their cause." Not only have they dropped their defensive posture, but their own assertiveness has become quiet, even urbane, in its detachment and indifference toward the "other morality." This withdrawal has aroused some of the greatest resentment and opposition since it is perhaps the gravest affront to an established ethic not to be taken seriously. To be defied is one thing; to be simply ignored and dismissed out of hand is something else. The spread of this more fullblown irreverence testifies to the fact that a good many happeners are managing to set up a life that is relatively independent of conventional society.

Another basic aspect of the hang-loose ethic is a diffuse and pervasive *humanism* which puts great store upon the value of human beings and human life. Adherents don't necessarily proclaim the rationality of men or their inherent "goodness," but they do claim that people are precious and that their full development is perhaps the most worthwhile of all things.

Killing is a heinous violation of this ethos and so is any action which puts others down, except under extreme circumstances. The most approved method of defense and retaliation is to turn one's oppressors onto the good life they're condemning and to help them resolve hangups which prevent this from happening. If this fails, one may attempt to "blow their minds," to shock their preconceptions and prejudices in some way and hence force them to open their eyes, to re-evaluate, and hopefully to grow. The

*13*

happeners refuse under most circumstances to employ the weapons of their adversaries because they feel that by so doing they would merely become like them. Instead, they try to transform their adversaries into fellows. The only really endorsed aggression is to try and force your enemies to become your friends. Only in extreme cases is putting down—the main strategy of the Establishment—even partly acceptable.

Ideally, the happeners do not fill the role of modern missionaries, though their practice in conversation and contact reminds one of historical attempts at persuasion and conversion. When approaching others, they welcome acceptance as well as adoption, but this does not imply that happeners resemble the adventurous, pioneering missionaries of established religious or ideologies. The few actual organizations existing in the happening world are there, first, to serve their "constituents" and, second, to espouse and inform.

This humanism, combined as it is with irreverence, produces a passive resistance toward the Establishment and the persuasive efforts of straights, rather than an active rebellion. The happeners are more transcendent than antagonistic; more indifferent and benevolently contemptuous than negative and bitter. Bitterness does occur over concrete immediate cases of harassment or "for your own good" busts, commitments, and putdowns. But it fades rather quickly again into the more general mood of simple wariness. The mood is not grim, although there is a diffuse paranoia toward the established social order which waxes and wanes as the scene gets hot and cools down again.

Another basic aspect of the hang-loose ethic is the pursuit of *experience* both as a thing in itself and as a means of learning and growing. The idea is that a great variety and depth of experience is beneficial and not at all harmful as long as you can handle it. This entails a heightened attention to the present ongoing moment and far less concern with the past or future. It also involves a mistrust of dogmas and principles which tend to obscure the richness of life. For this reason, they also often reject the catagorizing and generalizing which is so rampant in our educational system. Within the drug scenes, for instance, there is full awareness that LSD-25 can trigger "bad trips," for some people. But, again the fact of experience alone, whether guided officially by researchers or informally by "guides," overrides the application of a generalized rule about the possible detrimental effects of such drugs.

This courting of raw experience is what gives many people the impression that those participating in the happenings are without any morals whatsoever; that they are selfishly pursuing swift gratification of their impulses. And it is true that the unabashed seeking of experiences will frequently lead the seeker to violate what other people consider proper. But such judgments are one-sided. Although they see that swingers are breaking standards, they entirely miss the point that swingers are following another, different set of standards; so that arguments between the camps are in reality debates between conflicting ideologies.

As part and parcel of the importance placed on directly experiencing oneself and the world, we find that *spontaneity*, the ability to groove with whatever is currently happening, is a highly valued personal trait. Spontaneity enables the person to give himself up to the existential here and now without dragging along poses and hangups and without playing investment games in hopes of possible future returns. The purest example of spontaneity is the jazz musician as he stands up and blows a cascade of swinging sounds.

Another facet of the hang-loose ethic is an untutored and unpretentious *tolerance*. Do whatever you want to as long as you don't step on other people while doing it. A girl is free to wet her pants or play with herself openly while she's up on an acid trip and no one will think less of her for it. A man can stand and stare at roadside grass blowing in the wind and no one will accuse him of being the village idiot. If you like something that I don't like, that's fine, that's your bag; just don't bring me down.

The swingers, when you come down to it, are anarchists in the fullest sense. They chafe at virtually all restrictions because they see most every restriction that modern man has devised as a limitation on directions people can travel and grow. They feel that the irony of contemporary society is that the very restrictions necessary to curb an immature populace prevent that same populace from becoming mature enough to live without restrictions, just as a girdle weakens the muscles it supports.

Even clothes are regarded by some as mostly a nuisance and swingers have led the whole Western world toward simplicity and ease in styles and makeup. And over weekends and vacations, small groups will often go up together to back country retreats where whoever wants to can run around naked.

Without the fuss or the self-righteousness so common among Establishment liberals, the happeners have come closer to integrating the races, religions, and the sexes than any other group one can think of. A fierce equality is practiced among them, which is appreciative of differences in backgrounds and temperaments. Equality and tolerance aren't abject attempts to make people feel comfortable or wanted; they are dispositions that permit things and relationships to just happen without deliberate forethought and planning. In most happening circles, a Negro is not the recipient of conscious liberal acceptance, but an individual in and of himself who may or may not be a "good" person. Acceptance and participation is based more on how the individual presents himself within the context of the scene, not by preconceived and nurtured stereotypes about the way he is expected to be.

One's past is not held against one and one's reputation

is not spoiled by the fact that one might have served time in a prison or mental institution, had an abortion, or perhaps a homosexual affair.

This doesn't mean that the swingers will indiscriminately associate with anyone. Like everybody else, they choose their friends, their lovers, their acquaintances and the people they avoid by how well they get along with one another and enjoy doing things together. But they are less down on the people they don't choose to associate with than others generally are.

But the tolerance stops if somebody is stepping on other people. For instance, if a guy shows up in a particular scene and starts tooling around with other people's minds or bum tripping them just for his own kicks, several people are likely to get together and elect themselves to deal with him by busting *his* mind. And such a guy can quickly be shut out of virtually the entire happenings in that specific scene.

The ideal person in the hang-loose view embodies traits that are difficult to combine. Being as spontaneous as a child yet being sophisticated and worldwise; being fully self-expressive yet being always in control of oneself. This is the ambiguity of being cool. Being able to dig the ongoing present as it unfolds yet being able to get things done and maintain a competent life of fulfilled commitments and involvements. Being hang-loose from any constraining orthodoxy, yet being courageous enough to follow your own path wherever it may lead and whatever the travails it plunges you into.

The heroes are those who have managed to swing in some eminent way especially if they did so in spite of tough conditions. The distinguished outsiders of history, avant-garde artists, the leaders of unpopular social movements. The list of admirable people would include figures such as Aldous Huxley, Allen Ginsberg, Gandhi, John F. Kennedy, Fidel Castro, Alpert and Leary, and Bob Dylan. But such people are not so much heroes in the ordinary sense because, although they are much admired, they are not so much worshipped, and because they are critically discussed as well as fondly quoted.

The fact that swingers operate at least partly outside the Establishment and often even outside the law produces a certain admiration and sympathy among them for other categories of alienated and disaffiliated people, such as the Negroes, the poor, the mentally disturbed, the delinquent, the sexual deviant, and the peoples of under-developed countries. They do not necessarily approve of what these people do, but they do see them as victims of Establishments.

These sympathies, coupled with their tolerance and op- position to restrictiveness lead the happeners to take a "liberal" stand on almost every question and issue, from welfare measures to disarmament, to the legalization of pot and abortions, to racial integration and civil liberties gen- erally, to recognition of Red China and negotiations with the Viet Cong, to sexual permissiveness and progressive education, to socialized medicine and the exploration of space.

But most of them are not self-conscious "liberals." They take these stands for granted as the only reasonable and sensible ones, but they usually don't work within organized political parties to bring them about and they are not very happy with the compromising Establishment liberals who do. They support such men as Governor Brown, Clark Kerr and Bobby Kennedy only as the best of the poor choices available, all of whom are really more alike than different, and none of whom are really worth a good God damn.

But they are not pro-Communist either, although sympa- thetic toward revolutionaries in under-developed countries. They see Communism as at least as odious and repressive as the societies of the West and probably a good deal more so.

The hang-loose people are not joiners; indeed this is one of their defining attributes. They tend to shy away from any kind of conventional ideologies or fanaticisms, seeing them as unfree compulsions and obsessions rather than noble dedications. They regard those who are too intensely and doggedly involved in even such highly approved causes as integration and peace, a little askance and happeners will sometimes describe their own past involvements in these movements as something of a psychological hangup.

The villains in the hang-loose view are people and social forces which put other people down and hang them up, which teach people to be stolid and dignified rather than swinging, self-righteous and moralistic rather than responsible, dutiful rather than devoted. Those who, for the sake of some ideology, will set fire to other peoples' kids; who, for the sake of some ideology, will slap their own children into becoming something less than they might have been. The villains are those who pass their own hangups onto those around them and thus propagate a sickness, "for your own good."

This seems to be the still amorphous and emerging ethos which is the basis of the happenings we're concerned with. Admirable in some ways, perhaps a bit idealistic and innocent and even silly in others, still in the process of forming and changing, and creating many problems for everyone. And perhaps as inevitable, given current conditions, as the spring winds which stir its adherents.

And it is a set of ideals which, like all people, the adherents are not able to live up to. Sometimes when things get uptight, they betray themselves and each other. Sometimes, they can't resist selling out for a better package deal. Sometimes, despite their utterances they can become as provincial and arrogant as any tribesman who thinks he has the monopoly on truth. And sometimes they are driven by other motives to cheat and exploit one another. But such shortcomings are panhuman and can be leveled at any group including the United States Senate or the medical profession. And this should not obscure the fact that ideals are a potent social force which have a major hand in making people what they are. Ideals, aside from having a part in making individual attitudes, attachments and adjustments, also serve to categorize people as runners along certain tracks of life. What is today called deviant is tomorrow only eccentric. What harps upon and tortures the older ethics and ideologies, can eventually become an accepted, if not generally followed, belief system.

Like all ideologies, this ethos is sometimes used as a rationalization and justification. Irresponsibility can be excused as freedom. Apathy can be called being cool. Lack of dependability can be called spontaneity and so can boorishness and sloth. And virtually any behavior can be justified on the grounds that it is experience and will lead in some way to personal growth.

But then pointing out these blindspots may be a pot calling a kettle black for all ideologies are so misused and the misuse doesn't destroy the fact that they are also faithfully followed.

Those following under the banner of the hang-loose ethic are not of one stripe. Sometimes it is the spontaneous pose of a youth who is drunk on his own vaulting life-energy. Sometimes it is the final vision which has resulted from long training in some Eastern philosophy. Sometimes it is the whimsical realization that your hard work has produced a degree of comfort and success but that you're growing older and that things are perhaps just too uncertain to lay too much store upon the alleged joys of the future or the hereafter. Sometimes it is a temporary fling in what will prove to be an otherwise pedestrian life. Sometimes it is a later stage in a journey which has led a youth through romantic idealism, folksong clubs and science fiction, protest movements, a period of disenchantment, wandering, and psychedelic drugs while still in his teens. And sometimes it is the stony and even vicious hipsterism of the slum ghetto.

The hang-loose attitude is simply not a uniform thing. One can hang-loose happily or bitterly, stoically or desperately, wisely or floundering, as a posing actor or as a blithe spirit. Sometimes it is mixed with defiance; sometimes loving tolerance; and sometimes it embodies an indifference which smacks of callous unconcern for the fate of others. And sometimes it is tinged with the pathos of the feeling that in another, better world things would be different.

This ethos will have a somewhat different flavor in different groups and in different regions of the country. On the Eastern seaboard, it is likely to be more cosmopolitan and European in temperament. In the midwest it is more likely to be a reaction to the stolid Dirksonesque environment. In the South, it tends to combine the effete with the rustic. And in the West it is likely to be more gaudy and mystical. Among students it tends to be more self-reflective and among drop-outs it tends to be more starkly hedonistic. Among the lower classes it tends to be a proletarian disaffiliation, among the middle and upper classes it tends to combine the *Playboy* hipsterism with psychoanalytic self-realization. Among teenagers it is likely to be the following of fads, among youth it is more likely to be a search for meanings and recipes, among adults it is likely to be more cautious and more straight, and among older people it is likely to be hobbies and vitriolic conversations in the sun.

Among Negroes, Mexicans and Puerto Ricans it will tend to be more angry and physical and immediate, among whites it will probably be more sedentary and compromising and tolerant because it is more their society. Among Catholics it will involve "soul trouble"; among Protestants, a Nietzschean debate over whether God is dead; among Jews, an agnostic urbanity; and among the uncommitted, a search for alternative faiths.

In the urban slums it is explosive and a source of constant potential violence. Among middle class youth it is a source of scandals, a recruiting ground for protests of all kinds, and a susceptibility toward the milder, unharmful forms of deviance, and personal problems. And among suburban adults it is a careful but sometimes determined minority voice within the Establishment, and an "aw, come on!" ambivalence toward the Great Society bit.

American suburbs aren't the places of otherdirected conformity as Whyte and Reisman depicted them in the fifties. Perhaps they never altogether were. But the stereotype of the jovial empty-spirited organization man which may have had a good deal of truth a decade ago, now fits only a plurality at most—and a plurality that is no longer in the center of things, but off to the side as a disinherited conservatism.

In today's suburbs one finds a widespread diffidence toward job, background, and other external tags and badges. People are unwilling to think of themselves or others as merely the sum of their statuses and nothing more. A few years ago you might ask "what do you do?"; be answered, "I'm an accountant"; and say, "Oh, that's nice." But now you'd say, "Well, yes, but what do *you* do, who are *you?*"

Fromm's classic thesis that contemporary people are only using their freedom from the chains of tradition to package and sell their external selves until the package becomes the person and there's nothing left but a gaudy shell, is no longer so true either. In almost any neighborhood gathering, one can find plenty of evidence for a growing disaffection with external symbols (which were the main unit of currency in the heyday of the Sociable Ethic). Expressions of a certain distance from one's job and other positions and a conspiratorial show of fellow humanness have in fact become the newest gambit in advertising, salesmanship and interpersonal relations generally.

There is of course a good deal of the older ideologies still around and certain facets of them still ring faintly even among the most far out followers of the hang-loose view. Among those followers who are working within the Establishment there is still moderate disapproval of doing things just for kicks. Swinging should be "constructive," either by refreshing you so that you can return zestfully to the playful fray of your workaday world, or by helping you resolve psychoanalytic hangups so that you can move on to the next stage of growth.

And with a bit of pendulum swinging from the gregarious outwardness of the Sociable Ethic to the fierce individualism of our puritan predecessors, the current swingers in schools and suburbs are less concerned with courting the offhand opinions and tepid acceptance of the crowds they encounter. They are not immune to the smiles and frowns of others, especially people they like, but they are not enslaved by them either, and much of the time they groove along with an inner-directedness that would delight Reisman.

There is also an appreciation of affluence as with the Sociable Ethic, and in fairly sharp distinction to the self-conscious poverty of most of the Beats during the fifties. But this is more of a taken-for-granted that the world is full of material baubles which can be very useful, than a deliberate striving to accumulate them. The current swingers take national affluence for granted and only strive to have it distributed more widely and with less necessity of selling oneself to get a part of it.

The modern happeners like many of the things which our shopping-center society produces in so great a quantity, such as cars and clothes and stereos and prints and books, and they do not share the anti-television stance of the intellectuals during the last decade. But they don't want to struggle too hard to get them and they will freely loan and borrow them. So this shared appreciation of affluence shouldn't lead us to neglect what is now so different—namely that swingers have broken away from the high valuation of property which has been the cornerstone of every Western society since the Reformation and the rise of the middle classes. Property is not something designed to dominate an individual's life; it is something to be lived with and used, not as a focus of existence, but as incidental to the fact that humans are alive and dynamic. A young man, who like many others is only involved in some of the happening scenes, once commented, "do you realize that legally we can kill for the sake of property? What gives us the right to say that if a burglar is stealing a damned TV set we can go ahead and blow his brains out. Property, not human life, has become the most sacred thing in our society."

Along with the repudiation of property as something to work and live for, the hang-loose people feel less honor bound to fulfill commitments unless they are coupled with personal involvements and attachments. This makes them less dependable workers and spouses, and their lack of steadfastness creates part of their bad reputation in a society which still harkens to the Calvinist idea of duty. But swingers will not discharge their duties as students, workers, lovers, or citizens just because someone else says they *should*. "Should" isn't good enough unless it is coupled with "want to," stemming either from personal desire or personal convictions. Concretely, this means that they will break a law they disagree with, will desert a spouse or friend they no longer love, will cheat on a test they feel is unjust, will walk off a job they find odious, and will speak against a war they feel is dishonorable. The swingers will, because of expediency, often cool it by fulfilling obligations they do not feel personally bound to, but if they don't have to, they frequently won't.

Hence, an obvious strategy for those in the opposition wishing the demise of happening scenes and their tangential attributes, would involve making these people "want to" do something or discharge some particular responsibility. Sadly it is too infrequently recognized that unless those with the hang-loose philosophy are, at a minimum, tolerated, little progress in the above direction can be made. You can't call somebody a lunatic, beatnik, dope addict, or radical and expect them to jump to your beck and call. Regardless of how much reason and substance are part of the opposition doctrines, they will get nowhere until debate goes beyond mutual debasement and vilification.

In the hang-loose view, the main problems besides hassles with the Establishment and its blue-frocked representatives, are the personal hang-ups which prevent people from living as fully and spontaneously as they otherwise might. This is a more general and extreme form of the ideals of individualism, self-determination and self-realization which have been kicking around Western Civilization for several centuries and which have been such a prominent part of psychoanalysis. These ideals, when carried to their logical extreme by the swingers, however, put them in opposition to a good many of the rules and practices of the Establishment, which, like societies everywhere grants personal freedom only within limits and which labels those who go beyond these limits, deviant.

And this is the dilemma of the swinger. In the very process of attempting to resolve his hang-ups, he will usually move further outside the pale of conventional society and will become more deviant, immoral and dangerous in the eyes of the general populace.

Happeners are aware of this dilemma and spend long hours talking with each other about how it might be resolved. An individual solution is to become exceedingly cool—to develop the skills and habits to swing yet evade the eye of the Establishment by being discreet and by being able to play straight when necessary.

But this is only a makeshift solution, temporary and high

in personal cost. The longterm solution almost all swingers agree is to turn the world on. Their dream is to live in a world of beautiful people in which everyone grooves on their own things and doesn't interfere with anyone else in doing it. Where people will say "no" only because they want to and not because of fear or tie-ups. Where people don't make it their business to screw each other up over some decrepit dogma. Where children aren't stunted by "education" and "training" into growing up absurd, sad caricatures of their possible selves. Where people are free enough and fearless enough to grow their own trees.

If you think this dream is a little naive and foolish and fantastic, you are right. If you think it neglects and glosses over many of the realities of present world conditions and that it is a bit pretentious and unlikely, given the facts of history, you are right again. And if you find nothing good or true or beautiful about it, you can go to hell.

There is a storm of violent opposition to the hang-loose ethos and the behavior that stems from it. This storm of opposition seems to be of two kinds, and the first kind is moral.

A good many people feel that those participating in the happenings are morally depraved. Bratty overgrown kids crying for the freedom to play with each other underneath the streetlights. Arrogant but innocent youngsters who think they know more than they do and who are easy prey for dope peddlers, sexual perverts, and Communist agitators. A few more rapped knuckles, stiffer curfews and supervision, a few more jail sentences to set examples, and a stint in the army might make men (and women) out of them. But right now they're spoiled, oversexed, smart aleck brats who aren't worth their pay on a job of work and who are unfit to inherit our great country.

In the rush of controversy and opposition to what's happening, the swingers become *objects* for explanation, condescending sympathy, or condemnation. But because the happeners don't themselves own or have much access to communication channels for reaching the general public, the fact that they are active *subjects* who are in turn evaluating their evaluators is lost sight of. So their turnabout indictments seldom reach the ears of the general public, although they are widely circulated and discussed among the swingers themselves. When they are quoted by officials or the mass media, it is usually only to illustrate their alienation, willfulness, or delinquency. The quotes are treated only as graphic evidence of their sickness and depravity. Attempts, for example to legalize the use of marijuana receive the sarcastic and superior attention of smiling commentators on the 11 o'clock news. But, for those even partially involved in the drug world such activity is serious business that is a frequent subject of conversation, if not direct action. Although they might discuss it with a measure of frivolity, fearful of taking themselves *too* seriously, marijuana legalization has become a meaningful aspect of personal commitment and not some deviant's practical joke.

Parents and other concerned adults are discussing and fretting over what is becoming of today's youth and turning to each other, to experts (usually self-proclaimed) and to their officials for advice.

And youth are discussing and fretting over their elders and they turn to each other and to those rare experts and officials who are in any sense "where it's at" for advice. Restless and uncertain they are; unsure of themselves, of their beliefs, and of their futures. But they are more self-assured in their feelings that parents and mentors, neighbors and newscasters, officials and Presidents of the United States cannot be taken at face-value. They suspect—dimly or consciously—that their elders are not altogether honest, wise or competent to run the world and give advice, though many sincerely wish they were.

To the widespread charges that they are being immoral,

irresponsible, and irreverent, they turn about and reply: "Look at you, blowing up whole countries for the sake of some crazy ideologies that you don't live up to anyway. Look at you, mindfucking a whole generation of kids into getting a revolving charge account and buying your junk. (Who's a junkie?) Look at you, needing a couple of stiff drinks before you have the balls to talk with another human being. Look at you, making it with your neighbor's wife on the sly just to try and prove that you're really alive. Look at you, hooked on *your* cafeteria of pills, and making up dirty names for anybody who isn't in your bag, and screwing up the land and the water and the air for profit, and calling this nowhere scene the Great Society! *And you're gonna tell us how to live?* C'mon, man, you've got to be kidding!"

(This collage was made from a multitude of remarks dropped in a wide variety of different scenes. The remarks were usually reactions to specific events such as McNamara's proposal to draft the world or Reagan's promises of suppression, Dirkson's Biblical pronouncements or the sentencing of a youth for smoking a casual weekend joint. Ill-will is more of a temporary reaction than an intrinsic attitude among happeners.)

And the oldsters in their turn reply: "Well what are you doing that's so meaningful? Aren't you maybe on a hundred roads to nowhere too?" And the host of individual debates that go to make up the Great Debate continue all over our country.

The other kind of opposition is a practical concern. Who's going to be left to run the world if everybody turns on? This question bothers many people who are otherwise not so concerned about the morality or immorality of what's happening. They fear that nobody will be left to mind the store, to do those thousand-and-one routine but necessary things that keep society's wheels turning, her goods flowing and her children growing. Who will hold the world together?

Maybe nobody will hold the *present* world together. Who wants to? How much of it do we really need? How many of our proud items are only consolation prizes? Maybe a newer social order could evolve in which we would have the real things that we talk about on rainy nights but never quite seem to achieve?

The worry that the present social order cannot continue unless the happenings are checked is counter-balanced by the worry among happeners that the present social order may well persist in spite of their wishes and efforts to change things, and that the current social order at the worst may destroy the world in a thermo-nuclear light that would dim any prospect of an enlightened future. Here we find a true opposition and conflict between those who want to preserve the present moral order and those who wish to transform it.

Many among the older cohort worry whether today's youth are training and preparing themselves for the adult roles they are soon to occupy. This worry contains some validity, for many swingers are pretty unimpressive even judged in terms of their own values and ideals. A three year collection of *Wonder Woman* comics is perhaps trippy but it doesn't make the world a cleaner, greener land.

But the worry is also ethnocentric and historically arrogant because the young needn't accept or strive to fill adult roles as the oldsters choose to define them—and it might even be best if they didn't. On this issue youth *is* rebellious as it tries to revamp the more traditional conceptions of a "man," a "woman," a "career," a "citizen," a "human being." In their uncertain experimentations some swingers are probably stumbling toward what will prove to be more realistic and effective roles which may better fit the upcoming times.

Perhaps the most curious irony about the hang-loose ethic is that it is distilled from many of the highest ideals of Western man and our national heritage, carried out to their logical conclusion. America, is now, in a sense, confronted by a legion of youths who are trying in their own fumbling way to practice what generations of fatuous graduation speakers have been preaching. This emerging ethos which seems so heretical at first glance is partly a restatement of some of the highest ideals and values which the great middle classes struggled for during the Industrial Revolution and which have since served all-too-often as a covering rationalization for self-seeking exploitation; the ideals we learn to bend and compromise in the process of "growing up" and "learning the ropes" and becoming "mature." The irony is not that Americans have failed to teach the upcoming generation but that they have been perhaps too successful in their training and must now confront their fervent pupils.

## 3 / tripping out

When a movie or a passing girl or a sunset carry away the senses and the thoughts of a person so that he or she is no longer a dispassionate observer, but is carried along as a kind of psychic participant in the ongoing occurrence, the experience will most likely be described with the phrase, "it's a trip." A trip can be any happening that turns-on a participant and bathes him in the raw sensuous-emotional experiencing of the living world which lies behind our concocted word-screens. To trip is to be transported out of the ordinary and into some subjective state where you are directly connected with an unfolding present. Our workaday distinction between the individual and the other objects is blurred and the person is divested of his paper identity badges.

Tripping out is the most definitive and the most controversial thing that happeners are doing. Put simply, tripping involves the cultivation of direct experience, unmolested by poses and running interpretations. The trip is a subjective experiencing which combines the intense and the extraordinary, and this direct experience can be anything from the taste of an orange to a joust with the shadows in your mind. The ultimate in tripping is to reach a state of awareness so heightened and unmediated that it overwhelms and temporarily supplants one's ordinary conceptions and perceptions of one's self and the world. This state of sensory, mental, and emotional amaze is called "blowing your mind" in hip circles, but it has been called other things in other days. For some, at least, this is a beneficial experience resulting in self-insight, a realization of customarily obscured immensities, and an acceptance—in the existential sense—of the ongoing moment. But beyond, or rather before, any of these benefits, there is the fact of the trip one is taking as a pleasure and an end in itself. There is a feeling among many of the contemporary trippers that insight and self-integration can only be won after you have existentially learned the nature of pleasure and experience.

Knowledge and pursuit of such extraordinary states is older than history, and so is the evaluation of them as sometimes "good" and worthy of courting. Some peoples have valued them so highly that they were willing to employ drastic means, such as near starvation, the shock of torture, gruelling physical exhaustion, or the use of convulsive poisons to achieve them. Among the Plains Indians, one couldn't even become a "man" until one was able to flip out and see such "visions." And in many cultures, evidently including our own Biblical predecessors, the ability to reach such abnormal states virtually guaranteed the person an honorable and lucrative career. Such men and women were the mediators between that tiny bit of the Universe which the ordinary man knew and understood and the vast dark unknown which surrounded, and perhaps threatened to engulf it.

Tripping out is a new phrase then for an old and hallowed human experience. Just how a person trips—that is, what procedures are used, under what auspices, and for what purpose—has, however, always been of great moral, political, and hence legal concern. All societies from time immemorial seem to have been wary and equivocal about unregulated tripping because it held a good deal of danger for the fabric of the established community and its conventional arrangements for getting things done. Therefore, societies have always been interested in directing and limiting the trippings of its members to certain times deemed appropriate and to certain directions considered useful (or at least not so dangerous).

But because of its very nature, even highly supervised and ritualized tripping cannot be entirely regulated. And hence there is always a risk to the locally established dogmas which prescribe what is true, what is good, and what is beautiful, as opposed to the false, the evil, and the ugly. As Leary has suggested, there is always a tension between society and its visionaries which creates a dialectic cycle in which today's prophet is jailed for stirring unrest and his followers, a hundred years later, are jailing the next visionary. Since an inherent element in tripping is a partial transcendence of one's cultural and individual roots and preconceptions, it always involves a flirtation with the grave heresy of seeing through and beyond the local climate of belief and opinion. There is always some danger that the tripper will leave as a loyal subject and come back down as a critic or a revolutionary.

For reasons both practical and ideological, no society, therefore, tolerates unbridled tripping among its members. Most societies distinguish between "good" and "evil" tripping according to the prevailing local definition of these terms. The definitions they come up with will, of course, often differ markedly from the folks down the road and from later generations in their own country. But such diversity is seldom enlightening to anyone; more often than not it only provides the basis for holy wars and for the periodic rewriting of their history books.

Hence tripping is always a double-edged business of promise and danger for the individual traveller and for his society. If nothing else, the well-advertised fact that you're never quite the same person upon returning is, although an exciting prospect, also somewhat sobering to contemplate because even the most disturbed and dissatisfied among us cling to ourselves as we are, and because the known is less frightening than the unknown. From the standpoint of a working society (personified in family, friends, and acquaintances), every trip is a gamble. When the traveler comes out the other side of a rite of passage, a psychedelic experience, or even a summer vacation, he may be refreshed and "reborn" or he may turn away from everything he previously accepted and embraced (or at least didn't overly challenge or upset).

The rank and file have everywhere and always been in awe of the tripping experience and of professional trippers. Conventional people tend to attribute to unlicensed and even licensed trippers all of those characteristics he fears and disparages; self-indulgence, loss of self-control, sexual abandon and debasement, instability, irresponsibility—name your own favorite epithets.

In Western nations especially since the Reformation, the officials and members of mainstream society have looked upon such states with particular suspicion and disfavor, and have acted to curtail them, even in such natural trip-inducing areas as religion and love. The prevailing (and still widespread) practice was to dub ideas, feelings, and visions that differed markedly from the prevailing winds of doctrine as hallucinations. Even in religion and love, Western peoples have relied more upon stately rituals and upon commitments that are carefully negotiated and dutifully fulfilled. Our God was construed as a master engineer rather than a pulsing endless dancer. We have preferred the more somber virtues of dignity and self-control, and rampant spontaneity has been called immature, if not obscene. "Get ahold of yourself," we are incessantly told; "control yourself."

We shrink back from the immoderation of spontaneity except during the fleeting and troubled, but enchanted days of childhood. And even here our toleration is incomplete; we hasten to train our children in the somber virtues and we then employ this as our yardstick of maturity.

Our own society has developed within a Western civilization premised upon a series of moral polarities which are an insidious damnation of everything that surrounds tripping: spiritual versus voluptuous, nice versus wild, intelligent versus emotional, level-headed versus disturbed, self-possessed versus suggestible. How many times have we resignedly watched some mass media hero show us that he has finally seen the light and come to his senses by choosing the scrubbed girl with the righteous smothery smile over the unabashed and well-endowed companion of his supposedly wayward flings. "We pat people on the head for remaining frozen inside themselves. When you're straight you're bored, when you swing you're damned."

During the last few centuries the West seems to have held an unusually one-sided view of tripping. But throughout our history, even in the heyday of Yankee Puritanism, such "unAmerican" experiences have always had their subterranean followers and have flourished as a well established, if often harassed, countertheme. Such Dionysian traditions have been carried on in their most full-blown forms in cults and fringe groups at the edges of our society. But a dash of supernaturalism and sensuality and sophistry has spiced up the American Way all along—a dash not necessarily unwelcomed by a society that was wont to state its own craving to experience vicariously.

Waves from these more esoteric fringes are now washing over the entire society and our cultural mainstream is broadening to include them within its bounds. But this broadening is a violent process that changes contours, wipes away old landmarks, jeopardizes many peoples' holdings, forces old guides to learn new routes, and falsifies our treasured heirloom maps. And so politicians are accosted by both sides to act, newsmen are harried for *the* story, and opposing camps glare at each other across a chasm of ideological misunderstandings.

And now it seems that more and more Americans are cultivating a taste for the experience of tripping out by one means or another. Those coteries who use psychedelic drugs and a hand-tooled sensitivity to reach intense mystical states are but the avant-garde for a growing host of far more pedestrian and orthodox people who are coming to seek and appreciate immediate experience tinged with the mystical and bizarre for its own sake.

Human beings can be turned on by a thousand and one things, momentous as a martyrdom and small as a flowering shrub, common as an evening breeze and outlandish as an empathetic glimpse of a foreign way of life, as tolerated as the ecstatic pathos of young love or as condemned as drugs and perversions, as responsible as the selfless nurturing of a mother or as irresponsible as a heedless careening drive through a world of innocent bystanders.

The possible vehicles for tripping are varied. A host of drugs, yoga practices, isolation and meditation, fasting and physical exhaustion, finding soulmates, rhythmic dancing, intense vicarious identification, sexual eroticism, or a walk in the woods. The Western world is most familiar with such states when they involve religious fervor, love-madness and heroic drive; and they are only partly tolerated even here. Those who display too many states are likely to be committed as insane and will often, in time, come to believe this label themselves. Keeping oneself within the confines of moderation (again a hangover from the older ethic) keeps one safe from the stigma of this label; it's all right to enjoy something, but when you begin to enjoy it too much, there appears, as if out of the subconscious, the warning call to return to the "real world."

Every one of us has had some experience with tripping (even though we didn't use the term), has been turned on by a raging spring day, has been carried away by a melting love, has been lifted outside his empirical self by someone's creative artistry. Most of us let our fancies roam in dreams and daydreams and in fact, recent scientific evidence strongly suggests that such trips are necessary for the well-being of the human animal and that without them one suffers a "dream-deprivation" akin to sleep-deprivation.

Tripping is used in this broad inclusive way by those involved in the new happenings and by groups who have borrowed their jargon, such as teenagers and advertisers. But to the ordinary American, the word "tripping" has a narrower, darker meaning, of other people in other places doing something freakish to their minds. They've heard stories about philosopher guys watching the Universe dissolve into fragments and living fire consume their bowels and going back for a swim inside their mother's womb. And they've heard about beatniks and hippies wandering around downtown with vacuous smiles, and parties where everybody runs naked and does *everything* with everybody else who's there. And they wonder.

Just about everything that you hear about tripping does occur, at least once, somewhere. But what are the *usual* cases and which are the rare exceptions? Below is a half-typical trip scene.

It's a rule that no one is ever brought around to the apartment unless they're cool and each of the seven people here tonight is up on something. Everyone is known to Ron and Pauline (who rent the place) except Gordon, and Jeff brought him so he's okay. Ron and Pauline have been living together now for several months and they have become quite domestic. They're up on acid tonight.

Joints are being passed around from hand to hand as they're listening to Sandy Bull's something else rendering of the love theme from Black Orpheus. A fellow is stretched out on the floor with his head cushioned in a girl's lap. They aren't lovers; each of them has something going elsewhere. Maybe they will be sometime in the future, maybe not.

There are good surrealist reproductions on the otherwise drab walls and a pile of science fiction paperbacks and Marvel Comics on the floor. A board and bricks bookcase supports the stereo and a hundred or so volumes including many of the titles from "Great Books" lists, along with the works of Goodman, Miller, Hesse, Watts and Genet. Many of them were stolen from libraries and bookstores.

The record changes to Bob Dylan's "Mr. Tambourine Man" and Pauline becomes lost in the music. There's almost no talking; everyone seems to be on his own trip tonight. But there's a subtle atmosphere of warmness, that some would call psychic, about the place now and the people feel free. Gordon moves about the room looking at the pictures and out the windows at the life below. He picks up Heinlein's *Stranger In A Strange Land* and begins reading.

Ron is the veteran and even though he is bathing in the reverberating colors of his own acid high he brings himself down periodically to check and see that the others are all right. They say that he once sat by a girl who had flipped out of her skull for three straight days and nights and talked her down to where she again remembered who she was and was able to go out into the streets without being picked up by the Nabs. She had had a history of family hassles and psychiatric care and so most everyone had warned her not to take LSD. But maybe she had been right to go ahead anyway because she'd been less hung up since. Every once in awhile she still dropped by the apartment, her visits dramatizing her feeling that *this*, the apartment and the people in it, was a significant part of her life. Some would say that she had died and been reborn here; others would be more pedantic and say that the place had been an important phase in her development. But Ron and Pauline meant something to her that she could never put into words, although it was clearly expressed in the very soft and gay smile she wore while around them. This smile and a nod of the head was all they needed to communicate to each other; to say "yeah, it's all right."

The song is dissolving into its component notes and words each leading off into a hundred other places, yet it also remains a vast coherent river carrying Ron along and providing a place to return to from his side trips. He looks over toward that phase of the cosmos called Pauline and chuckles to himself about what's in a name. If he spoke the word she would flow up toward him, and he suddenly realizes that these human grunts do have tremendous power. Girl, with all the girl things and girl feelings; his girl; no, girl that he is temporarily connected with, sometimes. He wants to mix into this detachable girl-bundle of the cosmos with the detachable bundle of himself so there'd be just one bigger, stronger bundle. No, he just wants to visit the other bundle and then visit other bundles like the pool of Light up toward the ceiling. But he sees (would you?) that she's off on a trip somewhere within herself and he automatically adheres to the understood rule of not interfering with another person's trip, so he withdraws his movement toward her. He reflects, a bit wistfully, that both of them will have to be content with the always incomplete and only partial sex-thing later on tonight. Then he begins to wander along the windy beach evoked in the song, he recollects and begins to relive. . . .

There comes a sudden knock at the door, a pounding that seems to reverberate through the Universe, and everyone freezes. A look of pure terror comes over Pauline's face; caught and smashed, this will blow her whole future life, her mother shrieking at her, dropped out of the honors program, and ruins all around her. *Schmucks* strutting around and turning off peoples' lives all in the name of their own fuckups and their creepy dead gods. She throws her face into her hands and moans loudly, crying for all the sick sadness of the eons.

Swift as a panther Ron puts his hands on her and goes out to where she's at. "It's okay baby, let it go, I've got it." He tries to absorb the bad scene into himself and lead her back down at least to the level of the simple dancing lights. (Someday all the bad scenes will confront him maybe.) He brings himself down hard until the lights are only ordinary lights again and he is just a guy going to answer his door. "I'll take it," he says reassuringly to the others; and in a lower voice, "Oh, Fuck!" as a consolation to himself. All of this in a few seconds.

But it's only Stephanie stopping by to see what's happening this evening and the group welcomes her with a burst of laughter that is touched with almost hysterical relief. There have been rumors of impending busts now for several days so the people are jittery about knocks and noises outside the building, and Pauline's flash of "paranoia" didn't calm anybody's nerves.

The arrival breaks up the introspective mood and the people start talking together in the free and easy way of a group nearing the end of a shared voyage. Pauline cuts a brick of monterey jack cheese and Jeff, Gordon, Jenifer and Gary sit down at the litter-strewn kitchen table, eating the cheese and playing a game of imaginary bridge.

Gordon looks pensively at his hands. "I'll bid two dinosaurs." Jeff cocks his head. "I didn't expect dinosaurs. The distribution must be weird. I'll go three honeybears, I guess."

Jenifer says, "I'll go three anteaters."

Without hesitation Gary says, "Four wombats."

Gordon sighs. "I was hoping you'd come up with a wombat bid. I think we've got it. Six dinosaurs, and there's no need playing it out. You've got one wombat trick; the rest are ours."

They roll and pass around a couple more joints then spill outside. Jeff and Jenifer go to see an art movie; Stephanie goes off to the evening shops to try on dresses; the other guests pile into Gordon's car to drive over and see what's up with some other people; and Ron and Pauline walk down the moonlight flooded street toward a meadow that they like. Later tonight, most of them will find a TV set somewhere and watch Mort Sahl, the weekly favorite.

The odor of the smoked pot—"sweetest smell in the world outside morning coffee"—slowly dissipates in the now empty apartment and all evidence of the happening will soon be gone except for the memories of those who happened to be there. The stereo on the last chords of the Stone's "Going Home" will turn itself off.

But what's the worth of tripping anyway? One girl looked quizzical and answered back; "Tripping is tripping, something that just is, like jazz and sunlight. If you have to sit and ask what it's worth, you're out of it."

Although most people would be a little touched by such a direct and blithe response, it is not enough of an answer because it really only testifies to the speaker's wholehearted involvement.

"There are trips and then there are trips," a more seasoned veteran muses. "Some are just for kicks, some are a thing for connecting with other people, some are for digging things like the ocean and the movies, some are for diving way down inside and getting myself straight. Every one is different, you never take the same trip twice."

Most happeners seem to take for granted the inherent worth and value of tripping. There is a strong, but usually vague, faith that people are in some way the better for having tripped and most trippers fret only about the substance or intensity of their own voyages compared with others, or the rigid mentalities of straights. Those with a lingering allegiance to the Protestant Ethic (and this is

probably the majority) feel that tripping is a healthful anti-
dote to workaday pressures and an aid to personal balance
and growth. Those who are preoccupied with psychoanalytic and existential hangups feel that drug-assisted
tripping out is a means without equal for learning about
and living with oneself and the world. Lovers say that
tripping together is a more certain way of achieving that
merging of spirit which can transmute the world into a
magic garden and mere existence into LIFE. Those of an
artistic bent say that tripping is a wondrous way of en-
hancing their sensitivity and creativity. Others (and this
includes only a minority, contrary to the hysterical claims
from many newsmen and officials) tell you that riding
motorcycles, dancing, doing a sex thing, or even bopping
behind drugs is something else.

Some vault into the experience with the reckless abandon of a Viking; others enter into them with the cautious
calculation of a banker; and some find such uncanny
glimpsings so terrifying that they turn away with a shudder
and rush back to the conventional world, which is comforting because it is mundane.

Sometimes the claims of personal betterment are made
clearly and with strong conviction. "I never really related
to anybody in my whole life before my LSD sessions." "I
could never have written this poetry without acid." Others
are just as certain but less clear about the effects of tripping
on their lives. "I know, I really *know* that I'm more of a
person now, whatever the drug does." Others seem both uncertain and unclear about what has happened to them. "All
I can say is that life's different for me now. No, I'm not even
sure of that. Anyway, I saw some things that, honest to God,
shook me up. I don't think tripping's for everyone but I
want to know more, so if someone asked me, I'd have to say
yes, I'll be going up again."

Most trippers will agree that the psychedelic journey
isn't for everyone—at least not without preparation and

supervision of some kind. But they mean supervision by understanding fellow-travelers who are where it's at. They most emphatically *do not mean* condescending medicos (who would charge a fee many times greater than present black market prices), or scientists who stare at you like a specimen enclosed in glass (wouldn't that bum trip you?), or the majority of psychiatrists who teach you their own hangups, or state-licensed officials whose advertising-tutored sensibilities would be dismayed by a girl wetting her pants.

There are a few occasions when the worth of tripping will be questioned by those involved. A large number, when they first begin to use drugs and become involved in the happening world will have a soul-searching hassle with themselves over what they're doing. They are excited about the new scenes they're involved in and the new things that are happening to them, but this excitement is mixed with a guilty fear that they have been swept too far off the ordinary track and that maybe they are lost in the wilds. This mixture of enthusiasm and fright make the newcomer more or less tumultuous and unstable and uncool for awhile. But if all goes halfway well, the guilt and fright soon fade and are replaced by cool wariness or bland indifference about where one is at, relative to the main herd.

Whether the trips were really worth it is also likely to be questioned on those occasions when the traveler has collided head-on with some arm of the Establishment and has lost the joust by being dropped from school, committed to a mental institution, or brought to trial by the police. Even the most hang-loose veteran will have moments of doubt over whether the trips were worth all this. But the majority of them decide that it really was worth it, at least in the sense that they are not "reformed" by the bust. The point which parents and officials usually miss in such cases is that tripping isn't just a kick; it becomes a way of life like farming or raising children. And because it is a way of life rather than a weekend fling, it becomes a part of the person himself and can't be so easily abandoned. Those buffeted by the mainstream society therefore only turn away from the happening world temporarily in most cases.

(One thing which brings those who've been busted back into the happening world again is that they usually find that only their traveling companions give them much support and understanding during their travails. Those who handle their cases are all too frequently so condescending and patronizing and hopelessly square and lacking in human empathy, that the swinger returns to the happening world as soon as he can because he is returning to the only people who have proven to be his friends.)

On a milder scale the happener will sometimes run into scenes where he has to make some choice or compromise about his way of life. He may find that he must shave his beard and cut his hair to be placed by an employment agency, or a girl will find that a dress and hose make a great difference in how she is treated by university administrators. A steady job curtails following the winds of impulse and a straight but attractive opportunity in career or love may lead the person to forsake the happening scenes temporarily or forever.

And there is another, more personal occasion when the individual may well re-examine his former unreflective acceptance of the tripping way of life. This arises when the tripper has had experiences which have shaken or disturbed him so much that he approaches the prospect of future trips more soberly and carefully. Sooner or later the majority of those who trip will have a bad one for the same kinds of subtle reasons that all of us are bound to have some ventures that turn sour and attachments that turn bad and evenings that turn out unpleasant. The combination of inner moods and external risks, of mischance and setback, will practically guarantee that not all trips will be pleasant for even the most hang-loose and carefree souls.

But what precisely is tripping, people want to know. We have only been using metaphors to describe it so far, partly because the physiological nature of the process is as yet beyond our scientific understanding, and partly because it is such a private, subjective experience, like love or intense pain or happiness, that it can only be hinted at with words. Philosophers have pondered and debated the nature of subjective (phenomenological) experience for centuries. But widespread scientific and popular interest in the specific nature of tripping has come to the fore with the controversial rise in the use of psychedelic drugs such as LSD, mescalin, psilocybin, hashish, and marijuana.

Psychedelics are fascinating substances from almost everyone's point of view and a quite extensive body of literature on them has accumulated over the last two decades. If we exclude the mostly superficial journalistic accounts, this literature falls into two major categories. The first category is the philosophical and existential writings of those who favor widespread use of the chemicals; the writings on the subject by Huxley, Watts, Alpert, Leary, and so on. These writings are quite provocative but they are also partisan and they leave unanswered many of the questions which arise in the thoughtful reader's mind. Although they are illuminating and often highly insightful, they are also essentially persuasive arguments and must be evaluated as such.

The second category is composed of reports and statements issued by the more conventional scientific community. Since these are backed by the Authority of Science, they are taken to be the most valid information by newsmen, officials, and the general public.

But few people realize that these scientific reports are partisan too, and must be evaluated as such. As many eminent scientists (Einstein, Mannheim, Jung, Russell, Weber, Bentham, Mill) have themselves pointed out, all science starts with partisan assumptions and is, at best, objective only within their limits. Far too many of the scientific forays into the nature of psychedelics and tripping measure the voyages only by their own *pre-established* standards of what is normal, of what is stability and self-control, of what "reality" and a "reality-oriented person" is supposed to look like. No wonder that these measures "find" psychotic-like inner conflict and confusion in their tripping subjects —and in many cases, perhaps, help produce it. The questionability of the objectivity of these scientific statements is further enhanced when the researchers are a million miles in psychological distance from those who are currently doing most of the tripping.

The word "trip" is only a metaphor for an experience that is entirely subjective (although often triggered and carried and shaped in content by the ongoing physical events surrounding the tripper), just as a raging storm is a poetic metaphor that illuminates an internal emotional storm. In some manner not yet understood, tripping, however it is induced, partially frees the nervous system from its previous "programming" and allows it to operate in a more freewheeling, less prefixed fashion so that one's sensations are more intense and direct and one's thoughts and feelings are more open to new associations and re-combinations. The established patterns of the nervous system are hence shaken up so that new patterns can occur.

This suspension of the habitual patterns of the nervous system is the key to why tripping is a literally bizarre experience, and why it is likely to frighten the new voyager. He is experiencing in ways new to him and this newness is likely to occur wherever his attention falls. When he looks he will see things in their intricate complexity "as if for the first time." If he listens, he will hear the actual make-up of the sounds and the sounds will in turn bring to his mind a flood of unexpected associations and memories. If he thinks of another person he will conceive of them in new and different ways and will note things which have previously slipped by his habitual mode of thinking. If he looks at his own life he will see it in a different, broader, less defensive and hidebound way and he may suddenly become aware of many new things about himself. And if he looks around at his society he may see through things and games and cozy deals and arbitrary conventions that he was previously taking for granted as valid and natural. In sum, he is likely to see what he didn't see before. Needless to say this can be upsetting but it can also be freshening and educating.

The trip experience may also be bizarre because Western man is ill-trained and ill-prepared by his culture for such experiences. He is on new ground culturally, like a primitive man grappling to comprehend and use our higher mathematics and the logic behind them. It goes against our cultural grain so that the well socialized American may be terrified by the experience like a child in an unfamiliar house. Ironically, those who have been less fully Americanized and settled into the Establishment are those who are less socialized in an anti-trip ethos and are thus more likely to be successful venturers. And since they are also more attracted to the new and less bound by the old, it is no surprise that psychedelic drug use is most widespread among the young, the declasse, the estranged, and the outsiders.

Those who are opposing the use of trip-inducing drugs say that such loosening of the nervous system patterns produces illusions and hallucinations; distortions of reality and therefore a withdrawal or escape from it. They therefore refer to such substances as hallucinogenics (hallucination-producing) or even psychotogens (creating a temporary psychosis). Such terms, and more important, the judgment they carry, are used not only by outright opponents, but also by the more subtle opponents who wish to use and think of them only as chemicals creating curious symptoms in laboratory subjects.

Those who emphasize the beneficial and enlightening effects of such experiences refer to the chemicals that produce them as psychedelic (mind-manifesting). This terminological quibble is really, then, the symptom of a deep ideological conflict.

Tripping is always potentially disconcerting to the traveler because it shakes up the perspective from which he was previously seeing the world, and himself in the world. Even when someone's world view is grim, it is usually stable enough to allow him to move through his days with some coherence; it can be counted upon. But after the trip, the person is faced with what can be a very distressing task—rearranging his patterns and his views and his life.

The fact that tripping sometimes frees people from their somewhat habit-bound and encrusted selves is therefore double-edged in its consequences. This more direct and intense experiencing of everyday life may be coupled with an increased reluctance to fulfill those social duties which were contracted previously and the returned tripper may display an attitude which seems to border on amorality. It is true that such new reluctance is often something of a just indictment of these former commitments; schoolwork which is as much the learning of last generation's stereotypes as education; a job that really is an insult to human dignity when you think about it, a marriage that has come to be more deadening than fulfilling. But societies and institutions and families, as well as individuals, do have to keep going and the dilemma of responsibility to one's self versus responsibility to others can become quite sharp.

One of the main things connected with tripping is learning to "cope" while up. Coping is being able to do all of the ordinary tasks and duties and contingencies while under the influence of psychedelics and it is one of the main distinctions between being cool and uncool. The idea is to use the drug rather than be used by it, to be in some control of one's trips and to be as effective in dealing with your environment as you are when down.

People frequently have some trouble coping when they first begin to use psychedelics because the experience is so unfamiliar and they are yet unsure of what is happening. But as most any veteran "head" can assure you, and show you, coping with the world is a relatively simple act and, contrary to popular myth, one is still entirely capable of performing well under the most trying conditions once one has become experienced. And although psychedelic users will sometimes underestimate how high they actually are, like the drunk who insists he is sober, they are not physically sluggish or mentally stuporous, as people intoxicated with liquor are. To put it more concretely, a drunken driver is far more dangerous than a stoned driver.

The majority of the happeners use psychedelics only on special occasions, but a growing number go through their ordinary daily rounds while high. As one pot head commented, "I'd just rather be high, I prefer it. Everything's more enjoyable to me when I'm stoned, even things that the straights bitch about." A young female happener declared, "I wouldn't think of doing the housework unless I was high." Eastern philosophies have long asserted that all meaning and knowledge and beauty can be derived from even the most common of objects or activities. And without calling it a philosophy, this is the view held by the habitual psychedelic user. Anything and everything is a trip.

But all trips must end it seems.

Perhaps there is always an inevitable bit of sadness connected with sobering and coming down. But whether the trip involved pot, LSD, rhythmic dancing, sex, or a walk along the sea, there will inevitably come a time when the intensity of the raw experience subsides and the pressures from the mundane world intrude.

How one feels at the quiescent end of a trip will vary: a lingering euphoria which slowly fades away, a wistful melancholy that the sensory honeymoon is over, a determination to hold onto at least some of that heightened sense of aliveness during the coming days; a deep, even suicidal despondency at returning to the drabness of ordinary events; and occasionally, a sheer psychological refusal to come back.

If the trip happened to be a bad one the person will welcome the return to normalcy with weary relief. And even if the trip was good, he may be fatigued from it and ready to come down and rest. Taken altogether, the pathos of the bring-down seems to result from the discrepancy between the joys of the trip and the joys available in the person's humdrum circumstances. With some, this discrepancy is so vast that they may stay "out" and "volunteer" for "insanity" as the best adjustment to the conditions of their life. As Sullivan, the eminent psychiatrist, pointed out, this is not so much the sickness of an individual as the most reasonable action for a person caught up in a sick web of relationships and circumstances. The sadness of the bring-down can hence be the result of an especially good trip or an especially bad scene awaiting the person's return. As one frequent LSD user remarked: "I never have bum trips, only bum not-trips."

Dr. Timothy Leary—who, whatever else he may be, is one of the country's leading authorities on tripping—has suggested five dilemmas which psychedelic journeys arouse; a series of fears balanced against a series of yearnings we have paraphrased and expanded as a way of summarizing the psychedelic conflict. The terror of loss of rational control is balanced by the hope of transcending one's hidebound ways of thought and freeing oneself from programmed ruts. The fear of acting shamefully is balanced by the hope of casting off one's social fetters and behaving as one truly wants to. The terror of perhaps really seeing yourself is balanced by the hope of really finding yourself. The fear of disenchantment with one's society and one's position within it is balanced by the hope of insight into the inner workings of one's social environment and of seeing more creative alternatives. And the fear of discovering a "super-normal" realm so pleasant that one will never return is balanced by the hope that one can reach a level of awareness which will transform everything into splendor.

These dilemmas are the heart of the controversy now raging over psychedelics. Those who oppose are mostly fearful and very little hopeful; those who favor are very hopeful and not very fearful. The majority of Americans are wavering and waiting.

Opponents feel that psychedelic drugs have opened up a Pandora's Box of psychotic maladies and damaged lives and societal dropouts. More extreme factions claim that those who trip and those who even want to trip are sick—driven by compulsions which they are too weak to overcome, or else selfishly looking for kicks while decent folks have to work even harder to keep things going. The more moderate opponents simply feel that the drugs are extremely dangerous and that their use should be tightly controlled, for everybody's sake.

Most of those who are in favor of widespread nonmedical use will go so far as to agree that at least the stronger psychedelics are serious business. They usually become indignant when they hear stories about supposed plots to dump such drugs into a city's water reservoir or about a fraternity boy who dropped a cap into his date's coffee in hopes of making out.

But many proponents don't feel there is time to quibble. They disagree most fervently with the position expressed by one medical man who said, "What's the hurry? Let's just take the years we need to thoroughly research these drugs before we allow anyone to use them." But, the proponents argue, do our deadly societal games of atomic cops and robbers, of Black and White, of oneupmanship and onedownsmanship, really leave us that much time?

Some of the more contemplative proponents see the opposition as possessing a hysterical fear of what might happen if the masses were liberated, like the Church's suppression of the printing press and Ortega y'Gasset's aristocratic brooding over the spreading evil of democracy.

And, as is true of so much surrounding the current happenings, each of the positions is more ideological than empirical and the opposing camps are mostly talking past one another.

## 4 / who's happening?

When you ask a swinger "who's happening?" he will usually answer first and most easily with "who isn't." Not everybody. Not more than a small minority. Not people from all walks of life. Not Texas oilmen. Not the Pasadena Senior Prom. Not upwardly mobile Negroes who've split the "help your brother in the ghetto" scene. Not an Establishment that confines its immense energies to its own metabolic system. Not the cocktail circuit butterflies who chit and chat about civil rights and then "but . . ." Not the senior chamber of commerce or the junior chamber of commerce or the "man of the year" in Waukegan, Topeka, Vicksburg, Council Bluffs, or *Time*. Not the college president who lunches with alumni, trustees, legislators, businessmen, but never with his students. Not the contractor who gets caught (or does he?) cutting the concrete in the public schools he builds. Not Pearl S. Buck or Edna Ferber. Not Doris Day slaving away in her latest Gold Medallion comedy kitchen. Not the University of California budget. Not the proud father who ships his nineteen year old son off to battle in Vietnam. Not the "retire your life away NOW" villages sprinkled throughout the West. Not the people who worry about joining the "100 Most Beautiful People," or "if I do, what will He think" or whether a daring gown at Arthur's tonight will make it. Not the chicks shooting down millionaires for their own financial security and no one's happiness. Not Lyndon Johnson. Not the automobile exec who rises to demonstrate that making safe cars by 1969 would involve an unprofitable economic burden and not the people who listen to him and say "well, I guess 1971 is soon enough." Not society's censors, so terrified of a good screwing. Not the steel industries or selective service boards or the six o'clock news. Not the finance companies or Oakland's famous police force. Not the yachtsmen sipping drinks off Florida's Gold Coast, Long Island's North Shore and Los Angeles' South Bay. Not the cop who intimidates Mexican-Americans now that the Negroes have started fighting back. Not Walt Disney or the Cartwrights or McNamara or Ky. Not the father and mother who slap their daughter around with matching belt-buckles because she IS. Not the public opinion polls or rat psychology or the sociological survey. Not New York's stop and frisk law, nor California's anti-riot bill. Not those quaint old folks in the Marxist-Leninist revolution bag. Not the people who read *Time* and *Newsweek* to get both sides of the news. Not the socially retarded who grab up Berne's *Games People Play* in order to dominate and seduce their fellow men. Not the city council. Not the Christmas industry nor the Johnny Carson show. Not the good people who have convictions but no courage to follow them. And not the people who are always saying "ok" and never bothering to *think*. Not most people. Not everybody.

*Origins*

Like individuals, whole societies tend to learn something of a collective wisdom; a set of recipes and rules-of-thumb for handling the existential world and bending it in the direction of their hopes and images. For instance, men of the Western world have been struggling for centuries to learn to live in the kinds of societies which developed in the wake of the Industrial Revolution. And as Fromm,

Myrdal, Harrington, and many other scholars have shown, both the capitalists and the communists have responded by evolving into managerial bureaucracies with a host of problems such as human freedom and equality and grace, still unresolved on their ledgers.

But the forces inherent in industrialization have produced societies which are in constant change, so that their shape and substance alters even as their citizens are just learning to live within their bounds. Each succeeding generation is born into a world essentially new, at least in some important ways, and the recipes and rules-of-thumb provided by their elders prove to be at least partly outmoded—developed for a world which had already disappeared into history. The elders, already settled down into a style of life and partly blinded to the new realities by deeply grooved habits of thought, usually looked askance upon whatever innovations the young came up with for handling the world as *they* found it, and call them improper or even deviant. Consequently, each of the generations living together in contemporary societies like ours has grown up in its own world, and with its own views which are often in conflict with the preceding and succeeding cohorts.

From time immemorial, youth have been at least a bit evasive and irreverent toward the established order. And in America, there was an informal hell-raising tradition which flourished alongside our more sober church-going heritage. Beer drinking, petty thieving and vandalism, fighting and mild sexual forays have been a part of growing up for most of our ancestors, including the majority who became solid citizens.

But the current youth scene goes far beyond this earlier wildness. The youths of yesterday were fiercely and provincially American. Although they often bent the rules, they were narrowly patriotic and brooked no real deviations from the moderate American Way. Even when they broke the laws, they never went so far as to claim the rightness and morality of what they did. The hell-raising was also confined to certain times and places and was kept separate from the official goings on of the society. It was tolerated and even encouraged a bit when in its place, but it was put down swiftly and forcefully when it overstepped its appointed bounds. The present happenings however are neither so ethnocentric nor so cloistered.

What's happening is generational in that the younger segments of our populace are most actively, intensely, and outlandishly involved. The greatest cleavage seems to be this one between the generations; but the composition of the (often hesitantly and equivocally) opposing camps can't be captured with such a simple variable as age, as we will see.

Artists, intellectuals, mystics, and vagabonds, and millions upon millions of common anonymous people were the unknowing and unwilling experimenters who, in the act of living their lives, participated in this evolutionary collective learning. The tragedies were the historical cul de sacs; those whose attempts to meet the newer conditions failed, and who were swept aside as the times changed again. Men who had adapted to a frontier that disappeared before their eyes, small businessmen who didn't learn the economics of the discount house, individuals who didn't foresee or correct the disastrous provincialism of their ideas and values, and national leaders who miscalculated the true nature of events and swept their peoples into cataclysms.

The happenings we're concerned with in this book are partly the evolved distillation of this centuries-long process and partly the spreading influence of certain styles of living which first evolved along the fringes of our society over the last five or six decades. Both the forcefulness and the suspect legal and moral standing of the happenings stem from these origins.

There seem to be a number of things inherent in the

very fabric of modern society which form the necessary supports and underpinnings of what's happening. Without them, it probably couldn't happen—at least not in the form it has.

Urbanization—and all that usually goes along with it— is probably the major historical trend that has influenced the current happenings by throwing together large numbers of youth who can gain almost complete personal freedom from any direct control of elders by walking around the corner. The ease and swiftness of communications and personal mobility have the twin consequences of linking together the entire country (and soon the world) yet giving people the freedom of easy anonymity. Secularization, the fading of the force of traditionalism, and a pluralization of moral standards and the consequent blurring of certainties about what is right and wrong, have resulted in a more permissive and experimental (if also a more uncertain and insecure) social setting for striving to grow your own tree in your own way and with fewer constrictions. The growth of affluence and leisure have freed young and old from preoccupations with mere survival. (There is a very complicated, but high, correlation between the wealth of nations and the amount of personal freedom their members have.) Massive, almost free higher education has further weakened old traditions and once "self-evident" truths, and has made people a little more contemplative and a little less righteous (and self-righteous). And all of these factors together have made more of our populace more aware of the ways and views of other societies. Hence, the cultural base of America is broadening to incorporate at least echoes of what were formerly alien notions and perspectives. And the binding and blinding (but also comforting and supporting) force of sacred moral traditions and provincial perspectives has slackened.

The result of all this can be said in different ways; that people, especially youth, have fallen into waywardness or that they have been unchained from ancient shackles; that people no longer respect authority or that people are no longer tyrannized by authority; that people have fallen into amorality and irreverence or that they have risen from the sleep of the man with the hoe. Your view depends on where you're sitting.

What's happening among a good many segments of our populace seems, in part, to be the luxuriant stretching of a society that has more or less arrived at its collective goal of affluence. One senses something of a feeling that the holiday season has finally arrived, and, in almost every rank of society, there's the widespread idea that now's the time to live a little. This feeling rises above such somber items as international strife and unrest, interracial violence, the uneasy realization that not all our personal or national bills are getting paid, and the spectre of the mushroom cloud. Indeed, these darker themes seem almost to lend a desperate gaiety to the adventures and trips of the present moment, a lovely estate built upon a volcano.

The earlier decades of this century were times of tight-lipped Americanism. The wars and depressions and cultural growth along the lines established by our Protestant and industrial heritage kept us busy, but rather conservative and unreflective, as modern nations go. (During the same brief period for instance, Russia changed from a backward religionistic, absolute monarchy to a bureaucratic, socialistic giant and England passed from a proud but class-ridden world power to a largely bankrupt, welfare state with secondrate standing.) Our involvements in the wars, the world depressions, and the historical flux were often heartbreaking, but relatively slight compared with most other countries.

The Second World War was a kind of grisly coming out party for many nations. We emerged as the slightly reluctant but parochially self-confident leader of the non-Communist world. At home we began, with more than slight reluctance and much less self-assurance, to grow and broaden at a swifter pace and in more directions.

But even the decade of the fifties seems to have been something of a domestic latency period, a bit of rest, albeit uneasy rest, after the string of recent turmoils. It was a decade in which the old aspirations for material wealth and ease were more or less achieved and secured—at least for that top two-thirds of the populace who were first-class citizens. Sexual standards were continuing to relax, the inventory of "cheap" consumer goods continued to increase, and the trends of urbanization, secularization, and pluralization were continuing. And there were flurries along our society's fringes such as the Beats and the racial freedom groups and the proliferation of what were then called "cults," all of which made good news copy. But the face of mainstream America was relatively bland.

Not so however, the present decade. The major historical trends have swept forward and those "flurries on the fringe" have swept inward.

The direct beginnings of the current happenings are obscure, but one thing seems certain; they have always been rooted in the fringe. We have a subterranean history along with the conventional textbook one; a history of mystical and socialistic and bohemian counterthemes, of far-out rebels and sect leaders, of a declasse, of a precocious urbanity. And running strands of the current scenes lead backwards to certain earlier developments within this subterranean history. These early fringe prototypes were often different in content and in flavor from what is happening now but their traces are unmistakable. The immediate living pulse of Negro music, the grimly hopeful labor movements, the ethos of folk music, the occultism and esoteria of the "lunatic fringe," the realism and sophistication of art and literary circles, the campy glitter of Hollywood and the mass communications industries, and the urbane bohemianism which grew up in our giant cities. To these streams were added the more recent emergence of campus and teenage lifeways, the social protest and integration movements, the partial disaffiliation of a wiser and more experienced generation of youth, rock and roll and the themes implied and disseminated by it, and increasing echoes from European and Eastern cultures. Ways of living and styles of interpersonal conduct that were once confined largely to the fringe and avant-garde circles are now becoming more and more of a national pattern. And meanwhile the avant-garde are moving on to more experimental patterns, mostly out of sight from the conventional majority and in spite of sporadic, but sometimes brutal harassment from social control agencies. As is true with most social metamorphoses, there are many casualties, many benefactors, and a large number of people who are wondering just what is going on and what it will lead to?

This fringe background of the current happenings—the subterranean strand has never been very fully accepted or assimilated into mainstream Americana—largely accounts for their shaky moral and legal standing. There is a complicated, but high, correlation between the "fringiness" of a thing and its morality and legality in the eyes of the rank and file. A graphic illustration of this is the mounting pressure to legally curb the un-American (*i.e.*, far out) use of LSD and other psychedelics.

In sum, the current happenings are suspect in the eyes of most Americans partly because of their fringe origins and partly because our society has been fragmented by rapid social change.

*Spread*

Participation in the happenings is something of a matter of circumstance, although anyone can partake vicariously merely by flipping on the radio or walking to a newsstand.

There must be opportunity as well as wish and if constraining forces outweigh temptations, most people remain steadfast. Since most of us are ambivalent creatures, there must exist a good deal of local opportunity and support or an inordinate dissatisfaction with conventional circumstances to bring us to risk an existential leap into the happening world. Without such opportunity, without support and guidance, the person is most likely to remain an onlooker.

It is because this balance of temptations and constraints is always mixed that the happenings are not confined to only one age group or locale or education level. Even the older demarcation line between liberal and conservative misses the mark.

Neither participants nor opponents are confined to any one group. One can find truckdrivers, old farmers, midwestern schoolteachers, and southern ministers who are sympathetic, and some of them are participants. The relative proportion of those opposing versus those participating differs from one segment of the populace to the next, so that you can say that the young who are still finding themselves and the outsiders who live at some distance from the mainstream are most involved, and that older people who are already established and settled into mid-century American society are most opposed. But there is at least a scattering of both support and condemnation within all ranks.

This pattern of who's happening might be sketched out with statistics and differential rates. A million joints a day smoked in California and an increase of about five percent per month . . . Most happening innovations occurring on the two coasts, but more and more the West and spreading over the rest of the country in a half-year or so . . . The formation of new slang as telegraphic poetry and its drift upward into the high school buildings and the entertainment and advertising worlds, already dated and pruned of its nuances . . . The greatest participation among

West Coast youth, then the East, then Midwest, and the least in the South, with the degree of generational fragmentation following the same order . . . The spreading use of oral contraceptives by single girls of college age and down into the high schools . . . The movement Out in the late teens then back In in the late twenties . . . The differential spread of LSD use in different echelons; maybe ten percent per month increase among college students, three or four percent per month increase among the adult populace, and one percent or less per month increase among the elder cohort . . . Ten million or so at least one time smokers of pot.

But such figures give only the barest impression which leaves out the processes and linkages, the supports and impediments which go into determining who's happening. To convey this fuller picture, we begin with some features of the happenings.

Item: The happenings are a minority thing. Only a small fraction of the populace are actively participating even in such hotbeds as Berkeley, New York, and Los Angeles.

Item: Happeners neither own nor run the society. Because many of them are dependent upon conventional society for goods and services and opportunities—and often permission and spending money—they usually are forced to cool it, to tone down their defiance and accommodate their elders if they want to get things and keep the straight world off their back. Few swingers are so independent or uncaring that they can entirely thumb their noses at the rest of society.

Item: Most of what swingers are routinely doing is illegal. This is a compound process in which the acts are outlawed because of their fringe origins, and the happeners are then labeled sick and criminal because they've broken the law. Participants feel these are unjust suppressions, based on moral arrogance and enforced by authoritarians. And since laws pertain mostly to "crimes without victims" which involve no property rights or violence they are only sporadically enforced. Most often this takes the form of a periodic show of enforcement to satisfy what one policeman called the "pubic" officials.

Item: This illegality, combined with widespread participation, has led to a situation reminiscent of Prohibition days. Extralegal organizations (stirred by the classic American profit motive) have grown up to meet the spreading demands for marijuana, LSD, pep pills, abortions, and so on. The quality of such illegal goods and services varies from excellent to occasionally lethal as is true of legitimate commerce, and ethical responsibility toward customers seems about the same on either side of the legal fence. And in both business worlds, some unlucky people become casualties for doing no more than many others around them.

Item: As with Prohibition, the majority of those involved are otherwise ordinary people. With a few bizarre exceptions (endlessly trotted forth by newsmen in a string of mutual plagiarisms) most of them speak English and bathe regularly and are unrecognizable in a crowd photograph. Public stereotypes about weird dress and appearance simply don't fit the majority.

Item: The happenings are a spontaneous groundswell rather than an organized revolt. Those involved don't form any kind of solid front against society or against anyone for that matter. Even most of the vigorous opponents dismiss the charge that this is all a Communist plot and the organizations which do exist represent no more than a fraction of the happeners. And a good many of them know little or nothing of LEMAR or IFIF or SDS.

Item: The happenings are not an uninterrupted series of balls. They involve a variety of risks and vicissitudes and dreams that go awry, and most swingers feel the double-bind of trying to grow their own trees in the midst of an evershifting scene and in the face of harassment. Few of them altogether succeed, just as few Christians or married couples succeed in entirely living up to their vows. The bad scenes, bum trips, and uptight moments encountered by swingers include internal doubts and uncertainties, interpersonal hassles which of course plague everyone but are frequently more intense for them, and brushes with the Establishment. These problems make their social connections somewhat uncertain and their careers somewhat checkered.

A good many adults feel that virtually the entire younger generation is living in a social world that is hidden from their view and their ken, a world of shared meeting places and slang and understandings. This idea turns out to be partly true and partly false. Changing times and divergent interests always create something of a barrier between generations, as we have seen. It is also true that those youths who are swingers face similar circumstances and problems and do have many common interests and views. Because of these similarities there does seem to be a tenuous bond among this subgroup of young people which engenders an amorphous sense of comradery. This tenuous bond—the shared feeling of uneasiness toward the conventional world and the sense of being fellow travelers in the new world—is usually strong enough to support a common effort to insulate what is actually happening from the casual view of straight society and it provides some guarantee that one's private life will be kept private. And there is a shared jargon (derived from our society's fringes, particularly Negro ghettos and Greenwich Village) which embodies bits and pieces of the philosophy of those who use it, which provides shorthand communication, and which enhances a sense of togetherness.

But even these tenuous minimums don't always hold up. The slang miscarries and sometimes becomes a basis for making invidious distinctions about who is most with it.

And the defensiveness toward the Establishment which is part of the bond, is ironically also the thing which creates suspiciousness and concern about who is cool and uncool, who talks too much, who is likely to cop out under pressure, and who might be an undercover informant. In a matter of moments, a happening scene can be transformed from gaiety and contact highs to one of real uptight paranoia. Whether you're walking around New York's East Village in the atmosphere of seething racial antagonism and virtually unlimited police power, or driving along Sunset Boulevard under the constantly watchful eyes of the local "bike men," you can hardly avoid an uneasy awareness of yourself and whatever you may be doing. The fact that you can be picked out by foes as well as friends permeates all happening life.

The happeners live in a world on a string. Small favors are exchanged back and forth in a fashion reminiscent of small-town neighborliness and there is usually a good deal of mutual help and protection in emergencies, which is frequently extended even to those one doesn't particularly like. For example, the long-time resident bohemians around the Bay Area are not very happy with the more boisterous and amateurish New Wave of happeners that have descended upon their community in the past few years. But they still feel some kind of bond with them and interceded to put a stop to alleged police harassment of swingers along The Block in Berkeley.

One of the more interesting aspects of the happening world is its geographical spread in terms of making connections for drugs and sexual liasons, but even more frequently for friendship and acquaintance. It's an old story that when students go home for vacations (if they go home at all) or if they are traveling around the country they connect with friends from former days. On the West Coast, with its large number of college transfer students who go from school to school, it is not unusual for somebody at

Cal, for instance, to connect with someone at UCLA who in turn is already meeting with somebody from Oregon, or Washington, or Riverside, or any of a number of other places. This "connectability quotient" applies not only to students, but to hangers-on, transient youths, and working people on short or long vacations. A drug seller on the West Coast indicated this vague community attachment when he noted that of his steady customers (about 20 to 25), none would have much trouble making a score in at least one other city, many have connections up and down the Coast in the form of friends who can turn them on to a dealer or who may be dealers themselves.

In this carnival affair one quickly becomes a veteran. Today's hesitant newcomer, looking anxiously to others for assistance and reassurance, is tomorrow's older and wiser head who will spend some of his time guiding and reassuring others. In the emerging scenes around the country, one can find 20 year olds who are wise about where it's at and how to get there. Those who can't fit into the local scene, who seem used by rather than using such things as drugs and sex, who broadcast the feeling that their involvement is merely a gambit for some kind of interpersonal gain, drop by the wayside or into a niche where they're more accepted.

For the people who've been around, and usually they're over twenty years old, connections are commonplace, easily arranged, and looked forward to. They provide an opportunity for news and views to spread through the diverse happening subculture and startling similarities in expressed values, in speech and style, point up the fact that, despite the illegal nature of many happenings and the undercover atmosphere that prevails, the word still gets out and around.

But as with so many generalizations, this is only half the story. The new scenes also abound with instances of feuds, jealousies, of character assassinations, exploitations and betrayals, of discontents and jaundices, and restlessness. The casualties do occur and they are not simple cases of the wayward collecting the wages of their sins and good people being betrayed as some have alleged.

And the bond becomes more tenuous until it is negligible when we consider the entire youth population. The majority of young people, especially those in college, dress, think, and act like the girl next door or the young man applying for a job, and they tend toward stubborn moderation in all things. Looking neither to Left nor Right they are making a beeline for the suburbs from whence they came with only an occasional love feast and a few soul-searching talks for stopovers.

A classic example of "kind attracting kind" are those areas in most large metropolitan centers where happeners tend to congregate and settle. Be it the Av in Berkeley, the lower East Village (actually the East Side) in New York, East and West Hollywood in Los Angeles, Haight-Ashbury in San Francisco, or any number of college-oriented scenes, such as the Hyde Park area near the University of Chicago, the happeners are flocking together. The atmosphere is not like the gloomy retreatism of last decade's beatniks, as much as folks getting together for a big party. Here are the emerging economics of the happening world; the bookstores, record shops, ballrooms, coffee houses, and art theaters. Here are the gaily decorated walkup apartments and the incessant visitors and here are the slummers.

Almost as soon as such locales become established and known, they are invaded by the larger society. Happening communities these days resemble fringe areas of the past and are subject to the same waves of infiltration. The process starts with such innocuous items as tourist-catering coffee houses where visitors can sip overpriced coffee and watch the "weirdos at play" and it almost inevitably leads to campy high-rent structures. These units supposedly uplift the area by pricing out the most "undesirable" elements and at the same time permitting some "tolerant" portions of the middle class to live in culturally invigorating (fringe) areas. Incoming residents adduce some form of status for themselves; basking in deviant sunlight seems to impart a sultry social glow. What actually happens when the slummers move in, is an in-turn movement of the happeners out, to settle somewhere else, and the process starts anew.

Leading the happeners in their efforts to stand up on their own feet are the far-out writers and artists and musicians who have articulated their views and problems. But even more direct and concrete moral support comes from the free-spirited newspapers that have sprung up in happening scenes around the nation. As modern notes from the underground, these papers have a total paid circulation of thirty to fifty thousand readers. And, as many a subscriber can attest, his copy is usually read by several friends —sometimes even before he gets to the mailbox to pick it up. For many years, fringe people have relied on New York's *Village Voice* for chronicles and tabulations of outsider activities, while today, the "Voice" (which many felt had become tiresome, trite and too serious) has been complemented if not supplanted by a host of other journals that, weekly and biweekly, bring the underground the news of what's happening.

The three leading subterranean papers—and it is noteworthy that they are leading because they appear to be the only ones that have a decent level of financial security—are the *East Village Other* (New York), the *Los Angeles Free Press* and the *Berkeley Barb*. Other underground papers are printed in a sprinkling of cities across the country, often starting up and dying in a brief space of time. Confining themselves to news of interest to their special reading publics the papers rarely present the copy of traditional journalistic fare. Rather, they print (often with outrageously haphazard layout and "blood and guts" headlines) the news related to the news—or news which ordinarily wouldn't be considered as such by conventional media. Whether they're describing a Vietnam demonstration or a discussion of individual civil liberties in the face of police persecution, these journals do so with a flare and abandon infrequently seen in the modern American press. Without ever presenting themselves as a typical newspaper (that would be a fabrication for both the staff and the subscribers) they present their side of what's happening in society. Picking up causes right and left, they deem to speak for the underground in its constant trials and hardships. Being socially radical and not just politically radical, the papers reach even those who have withdrawn from outright political activity, who have now affiliated themselves with the revolution in social and interpersonal terms. Joking with their readers, never being too serious about themselves, the editors and writers for these papers nevertheless have been influential in formulating and giving voice to the underground perspective.

There are a host of informal, if uneasy, contacts between happeners and the more conventional. And these direct contacts—shadowy and abortive as they frequently are—are the innumerable bridges over which a traffic of mutual information and influence flows and which helps prevent the camps from becoming even more separated and antagonistic than they are now. Students play their phonographs at such a volume that their parents and neighbors must perforce overhear, and often as not older toes will start tapping. Busy citizens find themselves amused by the spunk and irreverence of the Beatles, Dylan, and the Stones. Store clerks, overburdened officials, and TV viewers notice something fresh and captivating about the long-haired girls who look back at them so candidly. And what the happeners say and do strike many as a little enticing and a little sensible, with the times a'changing and so much in doubt. Such contacts melt the negative stereotypes down a little and the fact that the happener is a person, even if he is a bit different, thus receives an undercurrent of acceptance within the conventional community.

Aside from their influence as paying customers in certain sectors of the economy, the happeners' strongest impact upon the larger society is through persuasion and example. In this process the teenagers are often the most crucial intermediary link. Today's high school students are the great American popularizers who adopt and disseminate watered down versions of the happenings and the ethos behind them. It is the high school students, more than any other group in our society, who penetrate and provide the linkage between both sides of our present ideological schism. In the records they play, the fashions they select, the slang and views they drop at the evening dinner table, they are the unintentional mediators and messengers. Little if anything originates and develops within this age-group but they comprise perhaps the most receptive audience and the most vocal carriers of new patterns and styles. And they are less disaffiliated and isolated from their elders than the slightly older corps of happeners.

Because the swingers have little or no say in running the schools, the mass media, public agencies, or the government, they soon discover that conventional people are necessary allies when they try to have a voice in societal affairs. For example, when Berkeley's proposed "urban renewal" project met defeat, it wasn't solely at the hands of swingers but was accomplished, in an informal sense, by the many civic-minded individuals attached to the same cause. Such (usually uneasy) alliances seem to be the rule whenever happeners become active in concrete social issues.

One reason why the happenings have been spreading more easily and quickly than previous fringe patterns is that they can be partially adopted and adapted by many other echelons of straight society. It's very easy to tap your feet to the current sounds, don the garb of the British mod, take up a placard in an antiwar demonstration, or send a contribution to the American Civil Liberties Union. Muted versions seem attractive and fitting to current historical realities and they help fill the void left by the decline of the Protestant work ethic and hometown provincialism. And at the same time, the muted adaptations are not so starkly oppositional or risky.

Aside from the teenagers, and the entertainment industries, the place where this partial adaptation is occurring most extensively is modern suburbia. Here, a modicum of alienation from the Establishment and from a taken-for-granted Americanism seems to be widespread and still spreading. The portrait of the suburbanite as a bland and extroverted conformist who has sold himself without even realizing that a deal was made, proves, as we noted earlier, to be an oversimple categorization that may have had some validity in the late forties and fifties but seems less and less true today. The suburbs aren't packed with secret swingers, but they are sprinkled with them and their more conventional neighbors now take job, newspaper headlines, traditions, commitments which lack involvements, and themselves, in far less dead seriousness than before.

This can be construed as a general rise in alienation. It could also be interpreted as a healthful and somewhat frivolous skepticism toward dolorous pronouncements and local mythologies. It seems to have aspects both of demoralization and of growing up. With a strange admixture of robust canny and world-weary cynicism (the weightings of which vary from group to group and region to region) they take less and less at face value. To a much smaller extent, they are haunted and liberated by the same double-edged unfettering of those more clearly outside. They have television sets and they watch them but sometimes their expression is quizzical instead of rapt. They work at their jobs but over an evening drink will express the realization that they are playing games. They barbecue and drink martinis and covet their neighbors wives and raise their children according to Spock, but they do these and other such things with a theatrical whimsey that shows a certain dissociation from them—a kind of diffuse declaration by the modern suburbanite that *this* isn't all there is to him. And when you talk with him a bit more, other things, probably surprising things, emerge.

These people would score fairly low on most alienation scales but they sporadically express and act out a subtly pervasive disaffection from the Establishment. Goals of exterior success and a degree of status are no longer taken as given, no longer accepted to the extent that they once were. On the whole, they are just unfettered enough to feel an uneasiness with the stock answers about career, marriage, school, children, conventional morality, and America's role in the modern world. Yet they are not sufficiently unfettered or knowledgeable of possible alternatives to really subvert their present way of life. In a half-desultory, half-desperate way they shop around for other possibilities. They buy and half-read a proliferation of books on yoga, health food recipes, classical handbooks on making love, the occult, psychoanalytic growth, protest movements, existentialism, and creative hobbies.

On a rainy walk or after a few drinks the most solid of citizens speak about the other things they feel they might have been. How they almost went to Lebanon that time. The crazy long-haired, artsie girl they came so close to marrying. (The only girl who laughed when the rain spoiled her makeup.) Just about the most beautiful piece of real estate on the Oregon coastline or the small cottage at Montauk Point they almost bought, it would have been the place to work on that book they've been wanting to write.

Sometimes these more vagrant feelings of jaundice with Americana are put into action. There is a relieved sigh when the TV set breaks down and a determination not to have it fixed this time. They go and attend meetings of some of the more esoteric associations in town and come home with literature-stuffed pockets. They call their real estate man to go see some interesting places outside of town that aren't so obviously constructed on the model of a box. They make discreet inquiries about job openings which sound like they would be a bit more meaningful than selling Tidy Rump Toilette Soap. They strive for that advancement after which they feel they'll be able to make some changes, bring some truth and poetry into the present sham.

But the kids prove more unmanageable without the TV and what else is there to do on Monday night. The meetings seem to become repetitious and a bit hollow; the country estate can't be financed at present and who would drive the children all the time anyway; the other job descriptions prove to be glorifications of mundane work and the pension fund benefits would be forfeited; the advancement brings more benefits but is no position of command. Nothing seems to altogether work and so they return to their rounds, but with a feeling inside that they're living on shifting, hot sands.

Faced with a changing and uncertain scene, aware of themselves as something separate from the sum of their activities, and surrounded with opportunities for a multitude of games, an increasing proportion of the current American populace seems to have resolved this dilemma: they have come to live in a way that expresses a bland diffidence and a restlessness. And this more freewheeling attitude seems to be spreading to more and more aspects of the contemporary scene.

But it would be misleading to simply conclude that the country is going bohemian. The "beatniks" have interpenetrated the straight world and conventional society has, in turn, gone a little beat so that the lines between hip and square, cool and straight, philistine and bohemian, are blurring and more people slip back and forth or inhabit the many-shaded areas between.

But too much of what is happening is simply too expensive and expansive for this superficial label of beat or fringie. Neither the swingers nor their suburban cousins repudiate the goods and services our economy produces and the virulent negativism toward tract homes, flannel suits, and new cars has faded. Instead, there is a more gentle and indulgent scolding of those who display their affluence as something to be prized. More than ever, Americans buy and buy, and items which were considered luxuries even a few years ago are regarded by every young bride of the sixties as rock-bottom necessities. But, perhaps because these things are now more easily obtained, and also, perhaps, because we've become more habituated to affluence, we are no longer so obsessed (pro or con) about our heaps of goods. And people now go to buy a major item with a canniness born of experience in the consumer carnival and with pained humor about its real worth.

Nor is the populace becoming alienated in the psychological sense of bitter estrangement, disphoria, and meaninglessness, The mood is lighter than this and the negativism and desperation which characterized many a bohemian of earlier generations is toned down if not completely gone. Groups of people still sit around and bitch about the times, the prices, and the government, but these into-the-night gripe sessions are milder than the vitriolic ones of previous decades and there is likely to be more good fellowship and less of a desperate clinging together. Today's happeners are not the burdened wrought-up revolutionaries of previous eras, seeking to change things come hell or high water, because they don't have the faith in some doctrine required for generating such fervor. And besides they're more comfortable.

Through the complicated processes of spread sketched

above, the happenings have moved from off-street privacy into the semi-public realm. On campus, around the office, and at the suburban cocktail gathering, people are becoming less wary about discussing what they are doing. Strictly public utterances still retain a stiff "for the record" character and one's actual behavior must be inferred from what's said about psychedelics, peace marches, sex and so on in even the more informal settings. Thus, although no confession, in the legal sense, has been made, communication and mutual sizings-up can occur. And this final outgrowth of the processes of spread, coupled with the mass media handling of the swingers, has brought the happenings into the arena of public opinion.

## Public Attitudes

The more settled echelons of our society look upon the happenings that are the subject of this book with the innocence which comes from scanty information, and with mixed feelings of sympathy, amusement, and concern.

The amusement seems to stem from the partly true, but also partly false, impression that the happenings are merely another generation trying their wings and sowing their wild oats. A Minnesota housewife smiles a little and says, "We used to have our times too. I think they have it easier than we did though."

Young people often *are* quite naive in thinking they are the first to discover inconsistencies in religious dogmas, the shortcomings of society, the deliciousness of secret sensuality, the pathos of injustice or the anguish and delight of consciousness-expansion, and they could learn humility from world literature. Young people are also prone to pompously overestimate their own savvy and sophistication compared to others, especially their mentors. But we've seen that a great deal of the modern scene is unique and that the happeners embrace a style of life unlike anything before.

Public sympathy arises from that freewheeling vagabond spark which seems to be buried somewhere within even the most conventional of us; that vagrant spirit which delights in daring rogues, which takes vicarious pleasure in the unabashed living of others, and which stirs with admiration for defiant acts, even when we disagree with the substance of the defiance.

Those who are actively swinging are, in this sense, swinging for all America. And in a more sober and levelheaded way many solid citizens are sympathetic because they themselves have doubts about some facets of the society the swingers are rebelling against. "I don't blame these people for looking at us and shaking their heads," said a fifty year old bookstore manager. "I think we handed them a lot of tough problems and I'm not sure what I'd be doing if I was growing up right now. I just wish they'd be more serious." An Iowa truckdriver said: "Everybody's screwing off these days. I can't do it myself because I don't feel any good unless I'm working hard. But I get a big kick outa hearin' about 'em, the drugs and shacking up together and givin' the big guys hell. Maybe the kids will come up with something good if they give 'em a chance."

The conviction that all is not well with the world seems to be fairly widespread among all segments of the populace and this conviction creates an undercurrent of sympathy and even encouragement for the swingers and protesters. "Let 'em go their own way. They're not killing anybody. Our government's the one that's doin' that!" said a woman in a Chicago bar.

But this sympathy only goes up to a certain point. One veteran swinger put it this way when speaking of the conventional world's sympathies: "It's a bag they're not in although they've probably tasted it sometime in their life. Their sympathy is with the flair and abandon because it's part of the human tradition. But when it comes down to the point of sympathy with the philosophy behind our scene, they can't and won't even pretend to be tolerant."

The concern is most sure to arise if someone close, like a son or daughter or spouse, is involved in the happenings. There is the worry that someone near and dear may be hurt or may be swept into the uncertainties of personal experimentation with drugs and sex and radical doctrines. Also there is usually the accompanying fear that there might be a scandal or disgrace. What might seem fascinating and amusing from a distance, becomes more worrisome and frightening when it touches closer to home. Numerous cases are recorded in the files of university and high school counsellers across the country of parents who reacted to the discovery that their children were smoking pot or using birth control pills by committing them to mental institutions or turning them in to the police in a last desperate "for your own good" effort to save them.

And aside from personal fears about kith and kin, many people are concerned in a more general sense. They see what's happening as a corrosion of the American Way of life, as a breakdown of the nation's moral fiber. Such people view modern dancing as shameless, clothes and hair styles as crazed defiance, literature and art as obscene and blasphemous, much of education as subversive and emasculating, corruption and deceit and perversion lurking everywhere behind the scenes both in high and low places. The fact that psychiatrists would diagnose such reactions as paranoid does not abrogate the fact that a fairly numerous group of Americans hold such views and act upon them. And not infrequently, this issue is becoming pivotal in political election campaigns.

"The America I knew is gone forever, I'm afraid. Everything's rotten," said a sixty year old Oklahoma real estate man, and a forty-five year old matron nodded in agreement. Such convictions seem to be most common among the older and less educated, and in more provincial regions such as the South, the Midwest, and the Mountain States; but they are certainly not confined to them.

Opposition to the happenings is a subtle thing often carried on indirectly and unconsciously. How can an advertising executive think that the work he is doing undermines the society's level of tolerance toward the different, the new, or, perhaps, the mystical fringe? Advertising people are proud (very often justifiably) of their ability to capsulize a situation, putting it in dramatic, if simple terms. At the same time, though, they are creating limitations on deviation from the terms they have established. Infusing the society with notions about personal makeup and care, dress, foods, and so on, advertising sets up the model and swingers who widely deviate from it are subject to stereotypic and oppositional labeling.

The happeners, taken as a group, are locked out of our society and they must either sneak in or make special arrangements with the gatekeepers if they want to visit for any length of time. One-sided press descriptions, parents who "lay down the law," a host of regulations on work dress, school dress, appropriate haircuts, welfare and compensation requirements, police administration, mass media jokes and governmental pronouncements have all contributed to the emergence of a negative stereotype of the happener and have created much of the oppositional pressure he is subject to.

Opposition is a fact of life for happeners. It's always around, always playing upon emotions and thoughts, usually cloaked in the guise of "help" and "treatment," and rarely respectful of another's feelings. The strength of oppositional pressures will vary from scene to scene; the West Coast is more permissive than the Midwest, California is more permissive than Oregon, and within California, the Bay Area is less suppressive than Santa Maria. And the happeners are a bit less secretive and paranoia-prone in the more relaxed milieu. But these variations are only minor fluctuations around the central, overarching fact of opposition. "You kidding, my parents won't let me come back to school here, not while *he's* still around. And I'll be damned if I'm going to live at home when I could be living with him." The battle lines between the generations often become crisp and visible. And consequently, a large number of swingers find the way of life they have adopted is not an easy creed to live by. They can strike no bargain with the gatekeepers. And so a good many sneak outside again.

But the concern of most of the public over the current happenings seem to be more equivocal and less sharply damning than this. An admitted liking for some of the music, some disenchantment with American foreign policy, and an interest in hearing stories about other peoples' experience with psychedelic drugs seem to intermingle with sentiments that maybe fun is getting a little out of hand, that we can't really afford these kinds of things in the "present crisis," and that an awful lot of weird people are running loose these days. Many will admit, when pressed, that perhaps if circumstances were different, they would be doing some of these things themselves, but they also say that this new freedom to do whatever you want idea has gotten out of hand. Along with the admission that some good things may be happening, is the uneasy feeling that something is awry.

The two general statements, then, that can be safely made about the public feeling that has grown in response to the spread of the current happenings are that they are equivocal and they are based upon scanty and often false information. People are so poorly and wrongly informed about what's happening because of its fringe origins and its distance and partial insulation from their own lives. Little of what they hear comes directly from those involved. And when it does emanate from the swingers themselves, it is usually either cautious and conciliatory, as when youths try to placate their parents, or as a defiant and in-flammatory reaction to having been put down.

Because these phenomena are not dominant or conventional facets of our society, all that most people "know" about them is what they have heard or read in the mass media. But too few realize that this mass media coverage is itself frequently secondhand and biased—written by newsmen who are essentially slumming. The elaborate and sophisticated techniques of presenting the results of such brief excursions produce an impressive and true-sounding, but often false, view of what is happening. Unfortunately, this manufactured "realism" is then in turn taken as the truth by readers and viewers who have little or no independent knowledge of the topic, and are therefore in no position to question it. A recent illustration of this process is *Life's* innocent and misleading coverage of the new psychedelic discotheques which missed the whole reason for the existence and success of such places (as action scenes for heads) and which has become a standing joke among West Coast happeners. There have been several instances in which happeners have sat around deciding what to tell (and not to tell) famous news crews who came onto their scene for *the* story. The coverage resulting from this compound put-on is then in turn widely quoted by other newsmen and even government officials.

(The reader is invited to try a little experiment to test for himself the depth and validity of our national news coverage. Pick a subject you are especially familiar with, or a newsy situation you have a good deal of personal knowledge about. Then read what a few newspapers and magazines have to say about it. Then draw your own conclusions about their coverage of stories and subjects you *don't* happen to have any independent knowledge of.)

It is paradoxical that as society wonders about the happenings and about who is going to take over if everybody drifts off into the multitude of scenes now emerging, there is a complementary worry in large portions of the general happening scene. Among these people—veteran outsiders and old guard iconoclasts and some leaders of protest movements—there is the *opposite* worry that those who should be actively rebelling and opposing the ills of the society will become so involved in indulging themselves that they will grow indifferent to the Establishment's doings. They decry the fact that the grim determination of previous radicals and bohemians is feeble or missing from today's rebel. Sometimes they charge that he is not a rebel at all but only a spoiled young punk who clamors mainly for "the freedom to play with himself underneath the street lamp."

Leaders of integration campaigns, free speech drives, civil liberties organizations, and peace movements are often speaking out these days against the widespread desertion of their causes by youths who have turned to swinging instead of sweating out social reform. They warn that if opposition to the established social order is emasculated by self-indulgent interests the entrenched industrial-political-military powers will rule the present and determine the future by default. They are worrying that the hang-loose ethic may simply be bringing us nearer a Brave New World of unfree bovine contentment.

This could happen. In fact it probably already has happened to some extent. Struggles between workers and industry have, at least for the historical moment, been replaced by cozy dealing; the declasse are becoming mostly passive wards of the state, motivated, if at all, only to win for themselves a larger share of the existing order. And if now that uneasy but immemorial coalition of youths and outsiders abdicate to go and play their own swinging games, who will be left to keep watch over history? We can't leave this task to the intellectuals and teachers in our society, say the radicals, because they too are domesticated servants, going after this research grant, that position of tenure, and a comfortable trip—all expenses paid—to some foreign land to give a speech or excavate some monument or teach the barbarians the facts of civilized life.

So, the radicals keep looking, keep hoping that somebody will be up in the crow's nest watching over society and history. But maybe everyone will. It may be that the hang-loose ethic contains a tough individualism which transcends rather than reacts to ideologies, which is less susceptible to the persuasions of dogmas and demagogues, and which is now largely concealed by the current one-sided reporting of it as an ethos of thrills and kicks.

## The Changing Times

Our thumbnail sketch of the development of the happenings and the accompanying growth of public concern over them, has left us with a host of questions. Why are so many people doing these things when they are illegal and dangerous? Why have the two phrases, "what's happening?" and "hang-loose" become almost the slogans of our time? Why do so many people turn onto psychedelic drugs? What's wrong with America that so many people become societal dropouts? And where is it all leading?

When there have been direct confrontations and conflicts between the generations, the opposition has almost always gotten the better of the swingers. But if the present belongs to those who now own and run the society, the future inevitably belongs to youth. Sensing this, many of the young happeners are biding their time, shrugging off the harassment, and playing along with the straights, in the conviction that they will eventually inherit the estate.

But whenever the times are changing and the very fabric of social life is in uncertain flux, there will unfortunately always be casualties on all sides; those who are hurt, those who become lost, and those who are left behind. Whether such casualty rates are actually higher during such shifting periods as the present than during more stable epochs, is a metaphysical question, difficult to answer, because many people "lose" by being stunted under a reigning status quo, and conversely, many people "win" new life and fortune during change. Whether the casualties or the beneficiaries are more numerous cannot be said. Such questions are mostly philosophical because, as we have seen, they involve moral judgments more than facts. They are also somewhat airy because what's happening *is* happening and cannot be stopped even in totalitarian countries. It can be stopped no more than a boy can bail out the incoming tide, because what's happening is a spontaneous grass-roots thing.

The increasing tempo of change is bound up part and parcel with what's happening, with the sharpening generational conflicts, with the white middle-class son or daughter who goes away to school, or even stays at home, only to become a "new" person, and with the casualties on both sides. Many fear that the accelerating whirl of social change will prove to be more than human beings can endure and that we will all be lost and eventually swallowed up in a churning cauldron of our own making. This fear is based upon some assumptions about human nature which are unproved and may well be false. A lesson of history seems to be that human nature is far more flexible than any tribe of historically local judges ever realizes. Certainly most people live at far less than their potential capacity (don't you) and it may well turn out that the flux of rapid change is invigorating for the human animal, not by tying him up in a series of knotty duties, but by letting him feel free, by letting him walk with bare feet on a dew-drenched lawn; simply, by letting him hang-loose a bit. It may be that breakdown during change results from a dragging over-grown rigidity and traditionalism, just as traveling is diffi-cult for a man in a straightjacket. And it may just be, say the happeners, that the past epochs of relative stability, the times so nostalgically sighed for by so many, have stultified the spirits who had to live through them.

## Implications

One wonders where all of this is leading to. A community of beautiful people? A nation of self-indulgent jellyfish? A dark carnival, as in the latter days of Rome, leading to eventual hollowness and horror? A craze which will wear itself out in a few years and be replaced by a new sobriety of religious or nationalistic morality? A new Renaissance of the human spirit?

Partly yes to each of these possibilities, partly yes for some people. But none will be the single outcome. Some people will be Buddhistic wanderers too beautiful and unconcerned to live very effectively in this or any other here and now. Others will pursue a kickster path, until overcome with weariness, and slide into some echelon of conventional society. Some will fall victim to the hazards of the road. Many will embrace some arm of the Establishment with the fervor of new converts. Many others will live their lives vacillating between several different social worlds, embodying the strengths and the weaknesses of marginality. And some will flower into those human beings who pace their times and the future. But which of these will predominate?

## 5 / the psychedelic drug scene

Dear Dad:

Dope . . . potacidspeedmetheshitboojointtrippedfreakfiend
. . . Timothy Leary is not a Lady Wrestler. And. Geronimo
wasn't George Washington's nephew. And that's not half
of it, like you said. Flip Out. It all runs together; indi-
visible, etc. etc. etc. from—if you can take it—the world
in which we live. Real. World. REAL WORLD. Our
world, not yours. The world of everything, dream dance
escape thought and blood. A machine has cranked us out.
And our father doesn't know how to stop it, much less fix
it. I know it scares you but it scares me too. It's not a NEW
thing (how could you call A World thousands of years old,
new?) but it is (could it be a hidden, old, familiar with a
new ring?). Yes. The Psychedelic World was what you
called it—bringing to your mind a different picture than
mine. "What is it all about?", you and others like and
unlike you ask of me and of others. Well, one thing, it is
*all* about; *all* around ever under and behind you and me.
I'd like to show you this world, this world neither of us
knows but the one in which I lovingly live. It's hold grows
tighter each day. My World capturing yet freeing me from
That World. You say it's a vice closing in on my rational
processes; a delicious piece of sticky fly-paper drawing me
until I'm stuck UPrightdownsideOUT. Your World. That

World. Ohhhh, yes! I know it unlike I know anything else. But I don't like it. *Let* me not like it. It doesn't scare me, for life has been cast naked in That World. We've seen its bared skin marred scarred tarred and feathered. My World. The Next World? Standing before me and scaring me and making me wonder about whether I *really* know and care about the what and why of my doing and activities in This World. You've locked us out of That World (presuming rather presumptuously that we had a wish to get in) with loving sternness and killing terms. There's a LOVE in MY WORLD for the new exciting land that was always far off the map in fifth grade geography. Things aren't always knowable and certain and stifling. To walk through it is its essence, so, Dad, let's TAKE A TRIP.

---

Stripped of any of its other meanings, the drug scene, or drug scenes if you prefer, is just what the young girl writing the above letter indicated. The drug scene is the central plaza of happening America. It is the main ring, the granite cornerstone with a bronze plaque, the center of the what's happening universe. It is the crossroads for conflicting ideologies. "That World" versus "My World." It is here, in the drug scene, that generational change in America most vividly thrusts itself forward; declaring that yesterday's rights and wrongs about things people should do are not the right do's and don'ts for the children who'll be tomorrow's fathers and mothers. We've already seen a partial reaction in our society to this outright declaration of independence. Legislatures are meeting and passing laws and approving penalties; medical convocations issue warning statements based on empirical research; high school, even junior high school students, see movies depicting the daring nonsense of playing around with drugs; and newspapers bring—daily in many cases—accounts of LSD-25 triggered hospitalizations and general disorderliness. Society has reacted—blindly say the drug scene adherents, correctly and justifiably say society's guardians. Those caught between the war of words and innuendos are trampled beneath those opposing parades of thought and emotion. The "reasonable voice" has been blown in the wind. But, both sides say there *are* no other reasonable voices, that their way is the proper path, and their faith the only true one.

Many attempts have been made to understand the current drug scene in America. Magazines and news articles presenting the facts are doing just that—presenting the facts about the price of acid (five dollars a dose in the West, a lot cheaper back East), the size of lids in Portland (Maine or Oregon, it doesn't matter, they still average less than the standard ounce measurement), and the mean age of the local campus' full time druggies (about twenty or twenty-one years). Rarely have these stories delved below—underneath facile categories of explanations. Our public, and it seems, regretfully, our legislatures are responding with fright. The message has hit home (despite many efforts for "objective" presentation) and the opposition is fighting back; sometimes with compassion (note the comparatively short prison sentences young *white* people are given in narcotics cases) very often with "for your own good" fury (how many kids have been beaten or in some way assaulted by elders?). Incredulously concerned—"I just don't know what to think," say many parents—yet clothed with despair about actually knowing "why?".

"They're so frightened," one young doper sighed, "they just don't know where anything's at in their world. We're shaking our brains a bit, so theirs get shaken too. Sure, they're frightened, I'd be scared if I were in their place and had this big, gaping, expanding, mind-blowing hole right smack dab in the ground below."

What is this gaping hole that has provoked both sides to scientific doubletalk and dervish mysticisms? There is something peculiar about the current drug scene, peculiar because of these reactions. What makes the adherents so adamant, so moving, so gracefully otherworldly, and even so divided among themselves in their proclamations? What makes the opponents lash out with such fear and anguish at the nature and increasing rate of drug use?

To the last question first: the psychedelic drugs are something really new for large industrial societies; cultures built on a "This World" axis. They're not opiates, addictives that can be "cured" even if it might take awhile. (On the whole, opiates are considered uncool in most happening quarters.) They're not pure physical stimulants like amphetamines and coffee or temporary mind-contracting items (like alcohol and aspirins). They're not even the lower psychedelic drugs which are tied to the bigger picture. The fear is the fear of the penetrating psychedelic; the fear of something going to the brain, doing strange and irrevocable things. A barber whispers in a customer's ear, "they're fucking with the mind, Bill. What do you do with a kid who's doing it?" This plea rolls across the nation on the heels of the fear. Psychedelics screw the mind; they're a foreign element introduced into internal order and constancy. It's Bad. "But is it?" they ask again.

They wonder. Does Timothy Leary really know what he's saying. Is LSD a fiery booster toward a sexual Nirvana, or is he putting everybody on? Are he and others like him strictly in their own scenes ("crazy" says Joe Citizen; "flipped out quite a bit" says Tom Drug), unable to speak for most travelers about a good many things? Can you really believe all the turgid accounts of drug activity you find buried on page twelve section two of your daily paper? "Isn't everything too simple, too black and white?" asked a midwestern matron scanning a statement by an opposition leader (in this case a Brooklyn, New York district attorney who has put himself in charge of an anti-LSD crusade). You hear it all the time—"It's Bad." "But is it?" they ask again. Still wondering and thinking, looking without ever having been there.

"Getting there is half the fun," claims the travel poster. But to the psychedelic world, being there is even better. It's a trip, a journey, an Alice in Wonderland visit to the near and nigh great world of zebra pictography. A dance under the strobe, a strong pulse beneath the sheets, the exciting coolness of a carbonated drink, deep blue notes by Miles, flowing words from Tolkien, and the searing hopes of a bright white world. William James, it is said, leads the quest for intellectual awareness (one particular quote is used so often, many drug people almost have it memorized) beckoning all to come to the joy of expanded, emerging consciousness. A kingdom of awareness above and beyond the confines of the gospel, the one and only absolutely truthful Morality. It's a world of fascination, mystifying splendor, captivating horror and geometry, filaments and dark roads. A world inviting for some—those who use the drugs they take—chilling and terrifying for others—the bum-trippers and the ones without an experience.

The drug scene pervades the whole happening world. Music gets called acid rock. Fashion is painted in psychedelic crimson. Dopers read their own books, not the literature of the unexperienced world. Politics become tinged with the happening ideology, anarchistic withdrawal. Whatever bag you're in (if you're not in the drug bag) your scene is outlined by its glow. It's *the* thing that's happening; from society's traditional outsiders (who often act as spokesmen) to clean-cut Fraternity Freddies. It's a bag that holds part of and is part of every other happening realm in today's America.

The world of drugs, though, isn't ideal. Its shortcomings —the burned deals, the oregano-weighted grass, the petty brotherly thievery—are the mirrored reflections of the larger society. They are not the same specific faults, but the similarities are too striking to pass by without a look and a wonder. Yet, even though it is at least a partial reflection of the other side, the drug world is a domain, an empire all its own. There are rules about this and rules about that. Lock the door; hide the stuff; pull the drapes; dim the lights. There are roles to play. The educator and chief missionary; the keeper of the goods and services; the dealer and his "dynamite." It keeps itself and its growth under a surprising degree of control, aware that drugs are a legal, if not a moral crime. It's a subculture of deviants, say the academicians playing with the typecasting function society has bestowed upon behavioral scientists; the deviants who structure their own world with special roles, rules, beliefs, and expectations. Just like the big world, but only a corrupted microcosm struggling to keep alive.

Going on the drug road is an escape. It's difficult to deny this no matter how you go about defining the turn to psychedelics. It's an escape from the reality of "That World," not to anything in particular, but to newer, worldly, living things in general. Psychedelics take the ordinary person to those places only far out artists, prophets, and mystics could formerly reach through natural highs (*i.e.* a natch trip). For most, dope is a kick. A kick to keep you going, to face the fact that in whatever way you choose there can be a way to meet the world, to charge out head on into experience. A time to revel in the glorious sensual freedom you've inherited from the strange *cannabis*, the lysergic acid diethylamide, the peyote, and the other mind-manifesting items in your local dealer's inventory. To sit back, lie down, or stand up to the floating arrogance of a contentment, aware that a downing will eventually arrive, caring only to sense the moment and all that makes it up. Is this the key to the popularity of the psychedelic high?

What does drug use at any level indicate? Is there something central and general about those who use them? The answer is probably "yes," there is a core of characteristics and it blends with the essential parts of the hang-loose ethic.

At least in part, drug people are irreverent, tolerant, humanistic, spontaneous, and/or experience seekers. The power of social pressure is strong, there can be no doubt about that. But it would seem that something more is necessary before one can overcome the huge barriers that the public stereotype of narcotic use presents. This is not to say, on the other hand, that obvious forms of group influence do not have a part in one's introduction to the world of drugs. With an air of "how could I have ever thought otherwise" a pretty university sophomore declared, "Well, they looked like they were enjoying it. We'd had the standard lecture and talks in high school, where they were always supposed to be doing bad things; then I got up here and found them smoking and taking lovely walks under the stars and having fun and just not hurting anybody—even themselves. Y'know, the grades didn't go down the tubes or anything like that. They said why didn't I try it so I did and I kept on with it. I mean, should I give up a good thing, something that if it's doing anything it certainly isn't hurting me, just because some freak in the state capitol says it's illegal?"

However, social influences come not only from friends who use drugs, who say what a trippy thing it all is, but also from circumstantial forces of the larger society. From, for example, so-called permissive child-rearing techniques —letting the child go into the world to inquire, question and search for himself, cast free from the one-directional channeling of an authoritarian home environment. And, too, some drug use is a reaction, a blind rebellion against restrictive parental proclamations. Drug use reflects many influencing factors and therefore isn't as cut and dried as many would have it.

High school kids sneaking into the parking lot for a fast smoke between classes, bohemians nurturing the ashes in their water pipes, secret swingers dislodging their cache of pot from its place behind the dresser, artists tripping out as they paint, college students returning from a summer's

European vacation with the resources for a soon flourishing business, religious leaders looking for truths the Good Book doesn't seem to offer, hoods and hipsters looking for the pleasant assassin's boost before an evening hunt in their respective jungles. It's a turned on world in increasing numbers. The world of drugs and the ideology of what's happening roll along together; tied with a lover's knot say some, with heavy leg irons say others.

"Some of my biggest, most consistent customers are Greeks; surprising isn't it?" offered a college area drug pusher talking about his world and his business. "It's happening all over, man. Just the other day I was walking down Market (in San Francisco) and stopped for a light at Fifth. Well, just as I get about halfway across the street this dude comes walking by in the opposite direction, stoned out of his mind and puffing away on his pipe." The drug seller's world is one on the move; it's one that also has long, seemingly interminable waits—for connections, deliveries, phone calls, wires, and money. But his business is dope and dope is his business. He should be fairly bright, with an ability to bounce shifting figures over and over in his mind. A capacity to sell a product, and not the product itself, must be considered an asset. In the long run, your personality helps attract (or send away) customers—good, clean customers with money in front and no narco's behind. You get to see your world; you get to intrude on the various scenes as you push your drugs, seeing the different styles as you go along—maybe "those multicolored paranoid peasants," or "the cats in the downtown bag."

"My fraternity and sorority customers?" queries the dealer, "Why, they're strictly on the once-every-couple-of-weekends scene. But when they go they try to do it up right. I've heard one story of two houses getting together for a Mary-Jane special. It's good for business when they go that route. Couple of dozen people can smoke up a storm in a night or two. Besides that, they're getting their kicks. Ya know, in the American tradition, I'd say they're getting their money's worth."

But these aren't the dealer's only buyers (if they were, business would be terrible) and there is small chance that they constitute his main group of associates and friends. You measure the dealer by his depth of involvements in the drug selling world. Some pushers are little more than carriers, a modern day Pony Express, discarding the product for someone with a larger holding, making his bread and butter from the few dollars he skims off the top. His is the most transient of the drug-selling life patterns. He deals in just about anything he can line up contacts for. Pot. Acid. Speed. The demand is always around and so are people who will try to match it with the most immediate supply available. These are the runners (and small-time peddlers) of the drug scene.

Hanging together, the runners compose the ever-present aspect of the drug world. Moving here and there, picking up on a bed, and getting their dope besides, they can be the picture of a special kind of freedom. A freedom of simple contentment, unglorified pleasures, and a general non-involvement with the world of ambitions and yearnings. Their travels sometimes lead them out of this scene, to the next level of sales which is one step above street-size transactions and curbstone bartering. The man starts dealing with increasingly larger sizes, with fewer people involved and more money as a return on his investment. As little as one hundred dollars can start him on the road to bigger things. To Ravi Shankar and James Brown on his own stereo and not another's. To chopped beef for dinner instead of a Nestle's Crunch as a snack. From the world of subsistence to the world of comparative plenty. Good trash, not bad. Clean sheets, not a floor. His privacy when he needs it, his status if he wants it.

Some drug people seek a night now and then for a relaxing break from the rigors of work and obligation. Others through time and practice learn how to make it a part of their ongoing lives. These people can use drugs—not just to stay high and tolerate the world, but as a means of shading everything they do with a euphoric tone. Speed to get going, to face some downtown bureaucracy. Backwards to soothe that uptight, "the world's a rubber band" feeling. Marijuana for reading, eating, watching television, doing housework, making love, conversing with friends, and even as a sedative to go drifting to sleep by. The people who use drugs in this fashion are naturally those most deeply involved in the drug world. They can afford what most consider luxuries. They can throw half-inch roaches out a car window, they can turn on five people a night, week after week, they can do this because, more often than not, they deal in one way or another. They simply like dope a hell of a lot and appreciate the bit of money that can be made from its sales. Some go from drug to drug, high to high, seeking the next horizon before the last has begun to fade. Others take their drugs as just another part of their life, if they're high they're high, if not, well, then they're just not high and they don't fret all that much about it.

These folks are the minority but they are also terribly significant. Except for those who completely withdraw from continual contact with others in the drug subculture while still staying high most of the time (they can afford this private luxury, either with a well-paying job or as a silent backer in a local drug ring), the full time head passes along the word on the drug scene grapevine, he tutors newcomers, and, most important of all, he keeps the scene supplied.

For most, again, the drugs are part of their lives, part of a useful trade. The man uses the drug, but no more than the drug is "using" him; tying him to an image, a picture of experience. This part of the drug scene is a commerce in concession. People fleeing "That World" for a kick, a fling, a moment outside, coming back, sometimes refreshed, sometimes hung-up. For others it's more than this. It's there like breakfast, lunch, and dinner, the toothpaste and the cranky wife. For those deeply involved, their decisions, their jobs if they have any, their tastes in music and food and literature revolve around their immersion in the drug scene. It's more than connecting a ki for $90 or bagging lids to raise some bread. It's being high all the time, taking work breaks or real world intermissions when the mood fits the need.

"Can I hassle it for six hours everyday, with only a half-hour off for lunch?" asks a full-time head thinking about adopting a part-time dishwashing career. But he's still the exception to the rule. The laws of scarcity regulate the drug use of most people. But turning on before an especially delicious steak and baked potato dinner, getting high on the way to a Spoonful concert, gathering around a fireplace to sip wine with the smoke and Sandy Bull isn't necessarily the full-time drug world, but a scene of relaxing pleasure, warm and jovial company, enjoyed by millions everywhere, each in their own fashion. Drugs, notably marijuana, have become a thing to do and there's no getting around this fact. The young, white, middle-class American kid has jumped in, feet first, for no less than "a momentary flash of a fleeting psychedelic spirit, a darting image of mind and nature bound and turning together."

In their spread, drugs resemble the flow of prohibition liquor; in their impact they are decidedly less severe, producing only a handful of sensationalized deaths, superb personal revelations by the thousands, and few if any cases of deadly comas or rampaging stupors. But the argument, so often used in drug scenes, "that such and such is really not as harmful as such and such" is actually a proposition that will get its followers nowhere. It's fine to point out the hypocrisy of a world that idolizes alcohol and cringes at the sweet aroma of grass, sanctions one, imprisons the users of the other. Yet, is something better merely because it's less of an evil? No. There must be something more than that. Something that brings some resolution to the act of escape.

These aren't children of the ghetto using smack to block out the horrors of their encircling, strangling, white man's world. These are the kids of the Establishment Liberals; the farmers, bankers, and insurance brokers; the children of the people who run "That World." It's this fact, too, that's bugging so many people. Not only are individuals screwing around with their mental cognition of the world, but they're the people we'd pick to run it once we passed on. These aren't the pathologically depressed souls of Harlem or Watts; but the sons and daughters of San Diego carpenters, New Haven real estate agents, and Detroit auto workers. Use cuts across the white world's arbitrarily drawn class lines. It's their reaction to a world gone sour, their search for something, just about anything, that will carry them clear of the shifting currents and plucky follies of "That World"; to carry them out, if only for an instant every now and then.

It's an attractive picture for many. For those ready to retire from an outright, face-to-face relationship with the other world. For those tired of hassling their mind over the mundane, the everyday, the uptight social morality. People are sitting up and taking notice—drug traffic among our youth is on the uptake with an effect that confounds and stuns the conventional society. The picture above, the image of relative retirement from the real world, doesn't fit with traditional concepts of youthful rebellion. It's not particularly bitter and misanthropic, nor especially violent in promoting its cause, and these rebels don't lead 50,000-man parades down Pennsylvania Avenue. Drugs are a quiet element in the happening world. Its pursuers would just as soon be left alone to trip away on their bands, their books, and their chicks (or guys). Not disturbing anybody, rarely looking like they had consumed in everydayworld type drink, they go about their business, their quiet rebellion. The publicity about the "drug puzzle" comes not from the followers, but from the Establishment—drug people don't need advertising. They never have and probably never will. The message is in the medium, says McLuhan; dope is both.

One of society's primary concerns is this rapid increase in the use (and abuse) of drugs. Their wonder and amaze brings them to look at the world, to understand and analyze it, and the opposition has discovered that, indeed, the drug scene can be categorized. It can be broken up and charted, slotted and chopped, registered and regulated in a four-square paradigm. Addictive (and physically habituating), non-addictive, psychedelic, and non-psychedelic. There's heroin, morphine, barbituates, and amphetamines, and others in the first and last classes. Marijuana, LSD, mescaline, peyote, the sacred mushrooms, DMT, and others in the middle two. Some cross-over along with the people who as "qualified dope freaks" jump back and forth, taking this, sniffing that, smoking that, and mainlining this. But don't be misled, for all these worlds overlap; the members intermingle, passing along traditions and rumor, dope and more dope. But, too, anyone who has used the drugs of the happening world, including the once in a while social high, has tasted the flight of a chemically-induced experience and has been in touch with a spirit. A sense of a journey into the night that has attracted mankind all over the globe for as long as we can put our memories to work. You've been there, however haltingly or hypocritically, you've still been there and it was a trip.

As the opposition attempts to gauge the drug problem (passing over several Establishment-approved narcotics such as caffeine, nicotine, chocolate, pills of all shapes and sizes, television, and alcohol) their attention is usually directed toward the "hallucinogens," as the psychedelics are now popularly referred to in the mass media.

Of all the drugs on the popular market, the items that have received the most attention are marijuana and LSD-25. Neither is new. The former is, in fact, one of man's oldest mind-meddler agents. In all its many forms, the *cannabis* pops up in almost every culture some time or other. It can be like a "physical wrecking crew" (hashish) or as gentle "as a girl's hand along the back of the neck" (marijuana). *Cannabis* is the mainstay of the drug world and all its scenes; it crosses the lines of specialized drug use, an old favorite standby of the long timers and the pleasing side-kick of the newly initiated.

The second drug, the one that has evoked the near deluge of furor, is LSD. Barely two dozen years since its discovery by a Swiss chemist, this drug, descended from the rotten ergot, has captured the thought and reflection of millions. Individuals who've experimented, who've used acid, have committed the unapproved act in our society—they've messed with their minds (the same naturally applies to users of the other higher psychedelics such as mescaline, peyote, psilocybin, and DMT). Few who have taken the drug, who have felt the bursting feeling of mental expansionism, will venture more than "it was truly an experience" when probed about the drug in an off-the-cuff conversation. Indeed, except for a relatively few trained professionals who've conducted and coordinated research in the psychedelic area without taking the drug, communication between those who have and those who haven't is verging on absolute nonexistence with each side talking past the other.

What exactly accounts for the widespread view that the psychedelics, the higher ones especially, have some sort of supernatural aura about them; some divine implantation into modern man and his creepingly civilized world? Why, for so many, are the psychedelics serious business— no mere tripping fantasy on flashing lights, but an important part of their efforts to figure themselves and others out? These are the people who started the whole affair, and whether or not they are replaced by the trippy-hippy they will always be thought of as forerunners of expeditions into a newly opened world.

How does one imagine the psychedelic experience? How does one describe a tormenting love affair or even a migraine headache to one who has never had either? It is a time when the senses come alive, when the fingers of your eyes dance on the movie screen before you, when the channels of your nose are filled with the fragrance of a budding rose, when the world and everything in it becomes a gigantic, lovable, universal community. As one head said rather simply, "Acid is another place, it's a place to be."

Undergoing sometimes searching, sometimes frightfully inadequate investigations, the psychedelic drugs are making people ask questions, all sorts of questions. Why are so many young individuals turning on with drugs? Is there something notably enriching about these mind-manifesting intoxicants, LSD in particular and others to a lesser extent? How should these items be used: only medically as some demand; as tools in psychological therapy; as guides through the everyday world of bills, letters, jobs; as catalysts releasing vast bounties of creative energy—or not at all?

Gleaning the proper use of psychedelics from the hundreds of pages of research, from unfolding accounts of personal experience, and from nurtured biases of media articles is no easy task. It seems apparent that, yes, psychedelics do induce something similar but not the same as a model psychosis. They do split the user from a "That World" axis. They do send him on a trip to a new and different realm of existing—some say a new and different world on every trip. They do present starkly startling contrasts between the world that's there and the world you're in when you take the drug. And, there's no getting around it, they can influence the individual to submerge part of his ego and the defenses he has spent years constructing. What happens?

Undifferentiated psychotic states, holding promise of eventual violence and self-destruction? Or, mediums taking the conventional self into its internal being, going through our game-playing to the reality of existence?

No real or absolute answer is available for these questions. There is so much mental turmoil involved in *any* analysis of psychedelics, such a conflict in the vocabularies of meaning for both sides, that any answer can be called a look through tinted glass. Few would deny there is a growing need for more controlled investigation into the use of psychedelics. And, undoubtedly, there does appear the need to put their use under some sort of control, no matter how minimal it might be. There are few—from Leary and Alpert to Cohen to FDA administrator Goddard—who would disagree with this. An argument arises, though, over the extent and purpose of such inquiries and controls. Should mind-manifesting drugs be put under international regulation, as some have suggested, in order to prevent their abuse by individual nations—to prevent a repeat of nuclear history? Should investigations be geared toward making psychedelics a legal product, distributed by the State, the millions of users members of small groups each with a certified guide? But as society presses for a solution to its present and growing problem, some things should be remembered; which should be recognized by drug opponents as subtle techniques often unconsciously used in the battle against drugs.

It's an old joke that statistics can lie as well as mislead, especially when the figures are kept by the poorest statisticians in the country—our police agencies. For years, state and federal officials tooted a similar horn concerning the relationship of marijuana to opiate use. Citing row upon row of percentiles and frequency distributions, they declared that marijuana use leads to the big stuff—heroin, morphine, opium and cocaine. Only in the past few years have some of these agencies publicly recognized the fallacy of their argument. The question is not whether heroin addicts, for example, have been involved in other drug scenes, but how many marijuana users graduate to the Big Time? The answer has always been "just a few," and the answer is no different today. What is the relationship between records of arrests, prison sentences, and drug use? Many police officials would have the public believe—but you know it really doesn't—that the general drug picture is one of increased use, though well under control. "Why," we're told, "just look at the hundreds of new arrests and convictions in the last few years." But don't these figures say something else? That drug use and drug traffic is not only on the increase, not only getting much larger in absolute size, but also that it is *not* under control. The largest busts for marijuana now amount to more than hundred kilogram holdings, not a few pounds scattered here and there. Three tons of pot was captured last year at the U.S.-Mexican border crossings, but anyone familiar with standard customs procedures, the Pacific coastline, and the ease of air travel between the two nations can just imagine how much wasn't nabbed by authorities.

The drug subculture is expanding, in many ways developing the attributes of a semi-organized primitive society. It has its capitals—Los Angeles for marijuana, New York and the East for cheap acid—its organizations and coalitions, traditions, and statuses that now extend beyond the little drug user cliques of a previous day. There is a growing sense of communication and camaraderie—picking up hitchhikers who look like heads, scoring some dope in a new city, carrying potent backwards for bum-trippers, even setting up a small drug ring to transport marijuana and LSD back and forth across the continent in search of higher paying markets. The drug world is here and there's no escaping the fact of its existence; wishful thinking and jilted statistics won't make it disappear nor will it answer the question whether it *should* fade away.

But what about all the people, the ones we read about in the papers and in psychology journals, the people who bum-trip, freak-out, or flip; the ones who go to the hospital for weeks on end, getting massive doses of thorazine to bring them back? There *are* more cases now than one year ago, than two years ago or ten. There are more because more people are using psychedelics, more people using them (abusing them, some would say) in a fashion the leaders never centered on, and more people getting bad stuff which, like its illegal brother wood alcohol, carries its harm in potent impurities and improper manufacture. Because no accurate records can be kept, and sanctioned investigations are increasingly restricted (thanks mainly to the underground nature of the activity and prohibiting legislative enactments), it is difficult to say what the probability of risk is in a psychedelic experience. A certain reporter claims to have found no "expert" who answers this question with a variance beyond one in a thousand up to one in five thousand. Takes at the maximum, with a few hundred in New York City hospitals, several score institutionalized in Los Angeles and the San Francisco Bay Area, and more all around the country, we could have upwards of a thousand hospital visits by acid heads in the next year. (Thought: does the high number of cases in New York indicate more than just proportionately higher use or is it an actual effect of New York's stereotype in the happening world—cool, but uptight, detached but paranoic?)

But there is more. Doctors and psychiatrists rarely see the successful experimenter. The one who dropped his cap or cube with pleasant company in a warm environment, the one who traveled with little or no troublesome effects. They admit this, but the press has passed by these methodological qualifications and gone straight to the headline making material in the scientist's summarized findings. The nature of hospital research brings them into contact, of necessity, with the bum-tripper, the one who's completely flipped-out. The present trend of public reaction doesn't leave much hope that a terribly important question will get a satisfactory answer, because we really need to know the odds of a bad experience, the odds of a trip right into Ward G of the County-Hospital. And we need to know how these odds can be reduced. If the drugs and their distribution were carefully scrutinized, would the bad-trips disappear? Has driving the psychedelic world underground reduced our chance of making something beneficial out of drug use? Almost certainly, yes.

We can't begin to answer some of the larger questions until these other problems are first ironed out. What must we do to search for and resolve the disenchantment with at least part of society that most drug use projects? What is the worth of a society that drives so many of its youthful heirs to another world; a world way, way beyond? What is the state of our ruling morality when it strikes out and slaps, then shuns those who show their disaffection with an assistance from drugs—why not find out the "why?", why not look at your own meanings and value systems for the cause of your own confusion and doubts? Look at your aging secretaries and your scurrying bosses who can't keep a routine day routine without an assist from the everpopular dex-bromo-phenobarb trio. Look and then think. Who should be on the defensive, drug people, or the rest of society?

This is the drug world, the world of questions and excursions, the world of propositions and hypotheses, the world that tells others that they really don't have *all* the right answers, the world where a quiet after dinner smoke of boo is no more harmful than a sweet liqueur, the world, say its inhabitants, that's really where it's at.

There is a chilling correctness about the drug scene's general approach to the real world's sticky problems and questions. "Is drug use really such a pain in the neck, such a sore on the body of society; is it *that* important, or are 'they' just missing an evident fact of life?" Drug people ask these questions to themselves, listening to the opposition over the telephone or snarling with their parents during a short stay at home, and they nod perceptibly: "Yes, that's right," comes out as a quiet mumble from somebody who already knows his reason for believing. In his last major work, the late Aldous Huxley, a frequent, guiding user of psychedelics, summed it up.

". . . widespread training in the area of cutting holes in cultural fences is now the most urgent of necessities . . . used to potentiate the non-verbal education of adolescents and to remind adults that the real world is very different from the misshapen universe they have created for themselves by means of their culture-conditioned prejudices. 'Having fun with Fungi'— that was how one waggish reviewer dismissed the matter. But which is better: to have Fun with Fungi or to have Idiocy with Ideology; to have Wars because of Words, to have Tomorrow's Misdeeds out of Yesterday's Miscreeds?"

# 6 / sex

Mostly on their own and in defiance of their elders, the more "liberated" members of our society have been evolving what amounts to a new pattern of sexual behavior and a new code of sexual morality. Like so much of what is happening today, the current sexual revolution is most characterized by its distinctive style—the approach of the individual toward sexual attitudes and the sexual act itself. The sensationalistic play upon erotic sex, so prevalent in the fifties and still with us in the sixties (responsible, for instance, in making the sex tease part of the American way of life), has been outgrown by many; largely young people dissatisfied with the tinsel values of America's commercialized eroticism. Because these patterns are in the process of emerging, they are still amorphous and uncrystallized. But already something of their particular shape can be seen.

A boy and girl talk casually several times while sitting at a table with other people. Perhaps he touches her hair once while he is getting up to leave and perhaps she touches his sleeve as she asks him about someone they both know. On a later day they may meet by accident and go for a walk together along the beach or perhaps they find each other at a friend's house. Afterwards, she sleeps with him because she likes him and because they were able to share other things. He finds her beautiful and, although he doesn't know her last name (what's in a name?), he knows that she too gets turned on by the sunset and Dylan. In a former decade she might have fixed him a cup of tea with the same grace and for the same reasons. Today she pulls back the covers and he might be in the kitchen rolling a joint. Maybe this is the beginning of a twosome or maybe it is only an encounter that doesn't survive the bring down of physical tiredness and the morning sun. But either way, the experience was a meaningful thing in and of itself, haunted by fewer compulsions from a frustrated or inhibiting past and constrained by fewer promises of the future. And it isn't inevitable; people who happen to be of the opposite sex will often spend great chunks of time together, will tell each other of their hangups and the dysentery they picked up in Mexico, will travel across the country together and sleep on one another's shoulder without any sexual intent or byplay whatsoever. Some will go to bed the first night they meet; others spend months in the same company with not a single sexual episode.

Acquaintances and friends become fleeting lovers, then acquaintances again; strangers meet and become momentary bedmates or soulmates, then dance off again to another partner and another scene. Those who stay involved with each other over fair durations of time—and this is still the majority—are involved in more ways and share a wider variety of things than unmarried couples did before. The traditional distance between the sexes has lessened. And they see more of each other under a greater variety of conditions.

But the new sex scene is not free love nor mass debauchery. More people are becoming more sexually experienced both in number of partners and in varieties of the act and sex is losing some of its sacred character along with many of the guilts and fears that previously hounded some who took part in non-marital sexual behavior. These people are reacting to the fact that guilt is something not always self-generated, but often created by parents and a society whose credo is that you *should* feel guilty. For many—more than ever before—sex is simply becoming another human activity. What's happening is that more and more pairs swing together just because they both want to. It is an easier, fuller, more candid, and encompassing style of relating in which the participants do more things together and become involved with each other as companions as well as sex objects to be used or romantic strangers to hang one's illusions and projections on. Partners come to know each other more quickly and more fully as fellow human beings with money problems, everyday habits, menstrual cramps, body deficiencies, and so on.

The newly emerging sex scene is partly a result of the major historical sweeps; the partial emancipation of women and youth; increasing secularization, urbanization, and mobility; and the dissemination of effective birth control techniques, especially oral contraceptive devices—liberators in any sense of the word. It is also the spreading of styles of heterosexual relationships which, as we noted earlier, first evolved in Bohemia and among the urban declasse. Perhaps it also reflects a sense of uncertainty about the future; a hesitation to live by long range plans in a scrambled and ever-changing time and a more intense sense of the present moment. A young man known to have lived with several girls once commented, "Why should I hang-up a chick, even if she wanted to get hung-up, when I don't really know where I'm going or how I'm ever gonna get there?" The day of the long-term romance where couples grew to know each other by exchanging daydreams and shy kisses has receded, just as it had supplanted the earlier widespread custom of marriage essentially by arrangement between families.

Romantic zeal (and innocence) is still rampant and of an evening one can find droves of young swains and maidens gazing about with that mixed expression of joy and anguish called romantic love. For that matter, partners are still brought to the parental home for sessions of mutual sizing up and parental disapproval can still carry enough force to break up many an ongoing affair. However, the growing financial and emotional independence of the young is continually gnawing away at the previously widespread norm dictating parental, and even familial, approval of the proposed mate. For many years, most people married the first person with whom they had a serious (but not necessarily coital) love affair, and they remained throughout their lives innocent of other possibilities, much like the primitive soul who subsisted on a diet of maize with only an occasional feast to break the monotony. And if you were a bit more liberal, and say you went to Harvard, you married, so the story goes, the second Radcliffe girl you went to bed with. These themes are not so predominant as they once were and the companionable style is coming into its own day. Less and less do couples represent graven psychoanalytically tinged idols for each other. Their sexual activities, including the waltz of courtship, are less dark Freudian wrestling matches and more tender intimacies and simple good fun.

Married life too seems more a swinging affair based on mutual involvement and fulfillment than execution of a solemn vow. Many divorces occur and these breakups still entail tragedy for a large number of people, but this doesn't necessarily mean that the American family or the institution of marriage is disintegrating. Those marriages which remain intact are probably on the whole more satisfying now that unhappy marriages have become easier to dissolve. Adultery's still around, but there's always been adultery and there is no reason to assert that it is on the increase, at least among men. The current change recognizes today's family and marriage function for what it is—the structuring of affectional ties between individuals. Crying about lost family purpose and meaning, says the ethos, is just that, crying over something belonging to another era.

The preliminaries to sexual intimacies are different from what they have been up until recently and the consequences of the fact that sexual intimacies have occurred have also changed. Rather than the measured steps of increasing physical contact which have prevailed in the past (and which were even given numbers running from one to ten in parts of England) there is now instead the preliminary of establishing some working level of communication which goes beneath the veneer of "where are you from," "what do you do," and "what's your major."

But the emerging sex ethos is not simply a matter of enjoying the companionship of others who happen to have 'different sexual equipment. Combined with this is a sometimes only semi-conscious search for the elusive essence of masculinity or femininity in one's partner. It is often semiconscious in that it can be inferred only from the choice of those whom one becomes really serious about rather than those one simply digs. It is elusive because the conventional models of man and woman have blurred and have broken down to some extent (as many writers have pointed out) and because what there is in the way of conventional models are more or less unacceptable. These models presume acceptance of things now being called into question—formal social grace, aggressive manliness, a ruthless drive for success, fashionableness, the personality sell, and so on. Each sex feels freer now to have attitudes, interests and tastes which were formerly the exclusive property of one sex or the other. Fewer things are thought "unmanly" or "unwomanly." Men can cook and sew, clean house, and iron; women can spout philosophical insights, tinker with woodcraft, and fix dirty carburetors. Thus for those with "liberalized" sexual codes it is positively consistent for a woman to admit forthrightly that she really does enjoy sex and for a man to fall in love with and marry somebody who's been to bed with a dozen other men. Some males go further, preferring girls who've had experience with others, shying away from virginity as a possible badge of coldness.

The sex scene is not an unremitted ball. Unrequited love, poor choices, and the disillusionments that troubadours have always sung about are still around. Girls still wait for the guys to move, though their invitations are more direct, less subtly clothed than in the past. And, as with romantic sentiment formerly, companionship and communication are sometimes unconscious or deliberate covers for starkly sexual goals. One of the common interpersonal measuring devices in the happening world is, of course, the other's view of sex and its place in life. Jill has sexual hangups and the tale manages to spread around. She's a virgin, though she really isn't sure whether she's right or not. The fact that she thinks she doesn't want to wait makes her defensive in relationships, often freezing up entirely. In some circles this becomes a confederation problem; in others a call for help, speedily dispatched by a close friend in whom trust is easily invested. Or, even, altruism with overtones of pure sex motivations on the part of males (as well, increasingly, as females) who ask "what's the matter?" while her interpersonal stock drops in the back of their minds. Jill is told about and is aided in getting birth control pills ("just go see this doctor . . . he's really cool about the whole thing"), which give a calmness of mind that will help her in living with her conflict about sexual behavior. Still, men remain hesitant, fearing preliminary frustrations and later over-involvements should a relationship develop out of some assistance they've rendered—"go ahead and groove with her, it's your sanity."

There's little doubt that the capacity to simply *enjoy* sex is greater among youth than among their parents; that they have fewer social and psychological compulsions and are surprisingly competent sexual craftsmen. A brutally simple law of learning is that competence increases with experience, and young people are starting to learn earlier than ever before. Does this mean that they have become self-indulgent libertines? Or, have they recaptured some of the simple human capacity abdicated by overcivilized Westerners?

The development and transition of sexual mores has always been difficult, if not impossible, to measure and depict. People in this country, regardless of their liberalism about sex, are hard put to rise above deeply embedded attitudes about "proper" behavior. Sex, as opposed to either love or marriage, for many was discussed surreptitiously, if at all. And numerous researchers have shown that the degree of permissiveness (or suppression) of sexual discussion goes hand in hand with the prevalence of emotional problems. Things like sexual teasing and game-playing, perfected by the American advertising industry, and often a central factor in interpersonal problems, seem to be fading among swingers as the changing sex ethic emerges.

But how many young individuals really approach sex with a freer, unmitigated sense of enjoyment and a feeling of responsibility to the other partner? Work measuring such attitudes and related behavior has only lately begun and the studies of the past two decades seem surprisingly inadequate when we seek to know exactly what's happening. Generally, though, they appear to support what we've already said. And their data gathering experiences indicate that barriers to the discussion of sex have dropped, if not totally, at least far below their pre-world War II level. More study will undoubtedly take place and with our expanding appetite for sexual data they probably will be heartily received. The past year, for example, has seen the rise of *Human Sexual Response* to the top of best-seller lists, despite its ten dollar price tag and its often laborious treatment of the topic. And social scientists, lawyers, and humanists are once again delving into the field in search of

the level and type of activity, its actual and legal consequences, and the philosophical pertinence of sex in the
Twentieth Century.

Increased distribution of literature about sex, both psychoanalytic and medical, has sparked a fairly common and
open awareness of the subject. So much so, that an average
coed can recite the latin nomenclature for her genital system and specify their role in psycho-sexual traumas. When
two people find difficulty in their sexual relationship, it
rarely need be the same problem it once was. If it cannot
be faced and assumed and then handled, the relationship
collapses more often than not. Females today are increasingly aware that their independence of spirit and womanly
freedom can have an enormous influence on male assumptions of masculinity. In turn, the impact can be seen in the
sexual response, or lack of it, on the part of the male. The
blurring of traditional roles has created certain amounts
of personal freedom from the obligations of past, customary
bases of relationships, but at the same time it presents
problems previously unknown.

For many years, to a majority of American females, the
presiding sexual norm was plain: no sex until marriage
(and not much after). Its important corollary was also
simple: no male will marry a girl who is not a virgin. And
a new creature was created—the technical virgin who went
just so far but never far enough for a full sexual commitment. This permitted the male to roam and romp freely, to
garner the tools and experience and emotional outlet provided by the sex act, to be prepared to teach when the great
step of marriage was taken. Times have changed, but not
as drastically as many believe. Because of their previous
roles, and long established values about sex in and out of
marriage, females have acquired a general set of meanings
about sex. For the majority, it is still the Big Event to be
supremely treasured.

Waiting, or at least being extremely careful in the selection of a bedmate, has enshrouded the female view of sex with the posit that reward will come to every female if she is not free with her body and thus her soul. The meaning has been drummed so hard (*i.e.* sex is the most beautiful thing in the world and therefore it should be "saved" until marriage) that it has come into conflict with the even older Protestant ethic viewing of sex as a necessary evil and not a supreme form of human communication. Today the first view can be seen as stemming from the emergence of psychoanalytic theory in the Twentieth Century, but amidst our mild sexual revolution even this doctrine has undergone noticeable change. The change has necessitated a different outlook from both the male and female perspectives. No longer is sex so sacrosanct that it need be saved until the night after the State waves its wand behind the altar. No longer need the man feel compelled, even obsessed, with a marital tie to virginity.

Contemporary lovers may move from no contact to complete intimacy with a swiftness which shocks and disconcerts their elders, but these elders are wrong when they judge this to be nothing but widespread promiscuity. Promiscuity does of course exist, but it may be no more common than it has ever been and as a sixty year old woman remarked, "We used to wear a dozen petticoats and skirts down to the floor, but a few still managed to get them over their heads." Very few youths will simply have sex with anyone under any circumstances, just as few people will accept a dinner engagement with anyone under any circumstances. In fact, for many, the controlling norm has become: sex is fine as long as it is not promiscuous. This vague and general dictum carries with it the obligation to feel that the sexual act possesses, in and of itself, a fine meaning that it is another form, albeit a higher one, of human relations. Given the fact that females, when faced with the choice, can sanction premarital sex in their own conscience, they also tend to believe—somewhere in the back of their mind—that the man they give themselves to will also be their husband when pragmatic circumstances permit. Increasing numbers of young females are finding that sexual inhibitions, guilt, and frustrations don't arrive immediately after the first round of petting or intercourse. Sexual neuroses are not always springing up when submission to sex is first made—the philosophy being "why wait if we're going to be married anyway"—as both parties are pulled into a half-believing, half-deceiving "we will marry" collusion. These neuroses, that can cripple marital as well as premarital relationships, are rising up with surprising frequency following the pre-marital divorce. For it is after the first tense, adult affair that the realization is made that more than one man will have intercourse with her before she gets married. It is at this point that adjustment to the situation is especially difficult, and that the success of future intimate relations can hang in the balance. Many girls have difficulty realizing that the male has also been exposed to our mild revolution, some firmly holding the view that they won't go into marriage with a virgin. They see women today as emancipated from restrictions of the past in which physical love was a selfish item, a commodity to be bartered in interpersonal transactions.

"Bed-hopping," as some young folks call their free and easy approach toward sex, is one side of changing premarital relations. The other face of modern sex revolves around the couple that, as one college administrator sputtered, "is an indicant of the high level of off-campus cohabitation." What this particular observer was saying was that a lot of people are living together today in a fashion more open than ever before. This is not the master/mistress relationship of previous eras, nor the behavior of two working people in their late 20's. Rather, the emergence of the unmarried young couple heralds a state of unblessed bliss. Couples living together, sharing expenses, doing the dishes, the laundry, and facing the economic necessities any married couple must bear, are common on most college campuses. And, indeed, even in the big cities where work and play come together, "setting up house" is certainly not unknown.

Living together, as any couple married or not will readily admit, is not like shacking up for an evening. It is filled with the joy, the tension, the trauma, and the closeness of any relationship kept at an optimum degree for almost twenty-four hours every day. One fact too often passed over by observers is this: young couples are literally and physically together almost all the time. Their general life interest is the same, especially in college settings, and their social relationships so overlap that they are brought that much closer to each other. Normal, married pairs are usually physically separated for a good portion of their daily lives. The lines between business, sociability, and the home-life are developed early in the marriage, but these are the same lines which are foggy, if they even exist, for the unmarried couple in the college milieu. This fact of life helps explain the intenseness of many youthful affairs. The ever-present intensity offers few outlets for frustration and disagreement and, because the choice to live together has not bound either partner in a life-long commitment (although marriage is seen by most as residing somewhere in the future), the unmarried couple is able to exercise an amount of freedom from each other that is sort of a halfway house between matrimony and weekend affairs. If, for example, a particularly crashing argument has occurred, it is no trouble at all for one of the partners to call up an old roommate or friend in order to secure housing for an evening "away from home." More common behavior, perhaps, if an immediate reconciliation cannot be made, is a simple move to another bed or couch in the apartment.

When campus couples live together they grow to appreciate their mutual responsibilities, the most important being the difficulties of living full time with another individual. The authors personally know several cases in which a couple has gone on to marriage, usually after one of the partners graduates or assumes a level of security in his occupation. We are also aware of numerous cases in which a marital disaster has been avoided by a period of cohabitation. Many young people, if they believe in marriage at all, want to make sure about the choice and have found living together the best means of getting an overall picture of a relationship's future possibilities. "Keeping house" offers most of the joys of marriage (less childbirth, hopefully) without the binding pressure of a supposed life-long commitment. And conventional society might note that these pre-marital trials save the individual and the State the pains and social costs of legal divorce.

Yet, even with a new morality, questions and problems remain. What causes the discord and sorrow that are part of so many youthful relationships today, while, paradoxically, the total sexual environment seems to have loosened, permitting a large number of individuals to freely and openly participate in sex discussion and relations?

Without much doubt, youth itself is a significant factor in the breakup of young couples—from the time dating starts in high school (or earlier in some locales) to the time serious courtship usually begins in the late teens. Youth in its fury (a New York policeman chided a nineteen year old Village hipster with "you people really have a rough time bringing up us old folks") sometimes forgets that as an individual gets older he also gets wiser. An individual of eighteen obviously doesn't have the same amount (or kind) of wisdom that he will have when twenty-one. As we get older our values and meanings are reinforced and refined, sometimes changed. Our particular likes and dislikes undergo the same process especially in the area of our attitudes about sex, love, and marriage. These changes are the hurdles young lovers must pass, and many don't make it without stumbling.

A second issue the changing sexual ethic must meet is the "standard" psychological problems of the past. Young and beautiful, Diane has been the victim of a disastrous home life (one of the negative benefits of today's freedom to pursue happiness in and out of marriage); her anger towards her father, the image in which she "sees" him, comes to the fore in her dating and sexual relations. Though desirous of sexual intimacies, even espousing a model position in favor of the new morality and growing one's own tree, her antagonisms rush forth, frustrating (or, worse, castrating) the partner and tormenting herself. The problem is no less real when the male is defensively agressive. Both situations breed unstable, probably divorce-bound relationships in which neither party gets self-satisfaction or fulfillment. With a widespread norm that accepts extracurricular sex, but not necessarily the responsibilities that go with it, the problem we have long had, outlined above, is multiplied many times over. What we have described here is only one of the many common friction-producing forces in human relationships. Others abound and there is little to lead us to believe they will disappear in a few years, if ever. (Possessive love as a neurotic attachment is an aspect of human relationships that's been around since time began. Few prophets would doubt that it is here to stay.) Some, those usually on edge to begin with, have already asked: "Is it needed? Is the new morality really worth it?"

The increased adoption of new sexual attitudes is bound to lead to some rise in normative conflicts within this nation. Personal mobility in this country is now widespread, and this movement combined with speeded communications bears two faces when related to American sexual mores. Individuals with attachment to changing, liberalized norms about sex must still face large pockets of "Puritanic" attitudes throughout the country. At the same time the word is spread, it arouses howling opposition. Our morality censors speak out against sensual dancing, symbolistic art, enticing literature, and almost everything else that in one way or another is part of the changing sexual ethic. Social reactions toward deviance from the sexual norms of a particular audience have never been known to be forgiving or comforting. On the contrary, those youths who come home from school, for example, as reformers of sexual attitudes must still face the anger of parents, who in turn usually ask, if not demand, the proper homage to the middle class "do's" and "don'ts" about sex and its aftermath. So, as the credo spreads and sinks into increasingly larger fractions of the population it also draws strident attacks from moral adversaries and advisors.

Regardless of the mental state of an individual, those who adopt and live by the reformed sexual attitudes are all too often called "sick," "depraved," or "perverted." Quite clearly, those who level such charges fail to realize they might be intruding upon another's personal code of ethics and behavior. If we were to follow statutory law as a guide to the state of sexual honesty in America, as has been indicated many times, we would be sorrowfully amiss in our conclusions. In over half the states in this country it is illegal to have intercourse in any manner other than with the male on top. Sodomy, as legally deviant sex behavior is usually called, is probably the most frequent and widespread crime in the United States. The past two decade's increased publication of "how to do it" marriage and sex manuals has been an invitation to partake in "crime" and "debauchery." Our changing sexual dispositions are a response to this hypocrisy and to other double standards about intimate personal relations. Those opposing the recognition of some new attitudes could even, in this case, be called the "deviant" few, for, in fact, it is the majority of Americans who harbor distaste for such statutes even though their disapproval is usually carried on in the secrecy of a boudoir retreat.

A specific response to the judgment that sexual behavior

is not a fair and adequate measure of mental health has been the development, too, of somewhat freer attitudes about homosexuality and bisexuality. "If one person wants to do it, if they find another attractive, who am I to say 'queer' or 'fag' or 'les'?" Punishment for homosexuality by consenting adults is one of the severest forms of misguided retribution; punishment for something intensely personal and private; a back lashing for behavior that, along with some other "crimes," certainly has no "victim." "I really dig it—who has the right to say I shouldn't? My moral code is my moral code and let's let it go at that," challenged one campus homosexual. As a matter of fact, although few have relations with others of the same sex (though it's more wide-spread than in the past), there is a growing feeling among hang-loose adherents that the homosexual should be free to follow the course he wishes, but of course without infringing on another's particular sexual prerogative.

The sex continuum, ranging from "it's bad and sinful" to "it's as easy as talking," is somewhere in the middle range today. Presentation of the sexual self is not really a matter of convenience or a "free love" ethos, as some would have it. It is a measured means of showing deep care and respect, a design to enhance and polish not culminate a relationship. The sexual inhibitions of the future will be found in those who have the greatest difficulty reconciling this approach with the one of the reigning generation in modern life. It is a problem of viewing sex not with some selfish values ("I've got to get my hair done at so and so's, do this and that, and Joe will jump right where I want him"), but as a documentation of feeling for another. With growing acceptance of an approach like this, it seems doubtful that motion along the continuum of sexual activity will recede; it is more likely to move forward, unhampered by the Protestant ethic of immorality or by pseudo-realistic doctrines of concerted amorality, both of which can easily detach meaning from all sex.

## 7 / the new politics

Political jousting by American youth has always been late and compromising. Unlike their fellows in other countries, who have for decades been toppling entire governments, American youth have concentrated on progressive minutiae; they've been aware that after their radical days they might move into some secure Establishment niche—"why fracture the system if you'll soon be part of it?" But indications are that great numbers of the New Left in the sixties never learned this particular response pattern and this specifically inconsequential role. They've taken a good, long look at past American radicalism and said, "that's not for me, I'm going out to do something." And they have and they will and that's what's happening.

Young people have rarely led the way toward the future they would rule, only occasionally have they decided that some share of the future must be shaped by them rather than be slaved to it. And with the advent of the modern social system, with its industries of production and consumption, with the onrush of science and the perfection of bureaucratic management, the young, especially the students, have been cast in the role of would-be inheritors of man's best works. What's happening today, in student and youth politics, is the realization of something which only sporadically flashed to radicals of the last one hundred years: that unless they take the ball in hand the game will still belong to the elders, to play and run as they please and it may well be called on account of darkness.

Radicalism in the sixties is out to have control of the ballgame; it knows that some vague hope for power and authority in the future will not do the job. Radicals want authority today, or at least to be in a position of enough significance to influence the disposition of authority by others. Simply forcing a few changes here and there with an applied use of power is no longer sufficient, for it is always feared that changes conceded by the Establishment are piecemeal and ineffective attempts at correcting social wrongs. Disparaging these radicals as diapered power seekers is no more realistic than charging them with a sophisticated political opportunism. Combining elements of both, the radicals are attempting to construct a political and social dialogue in which they will be full-time, accepted participants and not, as in the past, outsiders pounding on the door for an occasional review of their wispish thoughts.

The one fear that seemed to ride herd over young radicals of past generations has gone from the minds of today's activists. Namely, the fear that "unless we're careful, and play by the rules of the game, we just won't get anywhere, we'll be moving away from the patterns of influence." This fear has dwindled away. Whether or not any two people differ over strategy and implementation of radical doctrine, they no longer argue about the fact that sometimes, even often, rebels must leave the system, leave the game and draw some of the public to their own arena. Also, naturally, this offers a bright light of hope and provides common energy to conscious radicals of the sixties—not only is he ready to step up and take a swing, but there are others who'll join in and build a vibrant political community.

Some months after the famous Berkeley protests in 1964, a special investigating team, commissioned by a committee of the Regents of the University of California, issued its report, attempting with a large measure of fairness and concern to analyze the modern activist student: "For a few the opportunity to act in behalf of change is the essence of life itself.

"This generation of students acts from a dissatisfaction with the rate of change in American society and that dissatisfaction is pointed and intense. At the point of entry to the adult society, many students are deeply concerned about the commitment they can make to it.

"In the main, they ask not that the society be perfect but that they have the opportunity to help make it so."

Discussions of student political participation had to bear a new fact in mind as the sixties arrived. There were now more children in a nation of three-decade liberals, more students in bigger schools, schools more often public than private, than at any previous time in our history. And the results of what Harrington has called the accidental revolution—unintended social change caused by technological and scientific advancements—can be seen daily. As this accidental revolution unfolds, it casts a pall over any real political discussion, dimming the lines of difference between the Individual, Culture, and the State, and focusing excessive attention on the problem of simply keeping society going. New languages are emerging to measure a social order's ability to manage itself in a superbly "efficient" fashion; speaking of outputs and gross products, inflation curves and full-time equivalency units, the centralization and systematization of legitimate and pertinent areas of interest has impinged on America's ability to have far ranging conflict about goals and ends, not solely debates on overly discussed means. That is, there are only some things you can debate.

Rarely have American students possessed the flair, the abandon of youth groups in other nations; groups able to make or break governments, groups able to gain control of a university, or groups capable of attracting to their causes a broad, mass movement. And though these activities have been going on for decades in many nations, most Americans have become aware of them only in the past few years through stereotypic coverage of South American and Far Eastern student politics. But previous insurgency by American students has never met the test of time. Few remnants still exist of earlier youthful daring and until this decade, with its promotion of civil rights and international peace and disarmament, there were no contributions entirely detached from an older, adult movement.

Though a brief flurry of student activity occurred during the first two decades of this century, young radicalism was noted more for the ideas it proposed and the intelligentsia it promoted to debate and work out those theories. Thus, the Intercollegiate Socialist Society (Walter Lippmann was an early member) led into the formation of the adult League for Industrial Democracy, an organization designed to purify and disseminate Socialist doctrine. Their all but official absence today attests to the dynamism they failed to develop.

Depression, economic disaster, the promise of a welfare state, and the advancement of international war toward Western shores, formed the arena in which radicals of the thirties performed. The Communist Party, by then fully detached from any association with its American parents—the Socialists—sponsored its own youth group, the National Student Union. The Student League for Industrial Democracy was the Socialist youth organization. (The League for Industrial Democracy and its youth wing, sponsors of Students for a Democratic Society when it was founded in 1960, lost even this faint role in modern activism, when SDS dropped all attachments in 1966.) In addition, campuses across the country were the homes for spatterings of other groups.

Formed in 1935 as an answer to an appeal (mainly from the Communists) for a united front, the American Student

Union reached a reported high of 20,000 members. Proclaiming (when a consensus could be reached) various causes, the ASU tended to concentrate on an anti-war program. Supporting the English Oxford Pledge—which declared moral and physical detachment from future wars—and annual peace rallies, the ASU was constantly hampered in its efforts by divisions within the ranks.

Splits are common for American radicalism, young or old. Divisions are obvious today and it would appear that whenever there is revolutionary sentiment there will eventually develop disagreement as to the means of achieving the revolution. But the division of the thirties can probably be laid at the door of the communists who constantly put themselves in illogical positions as they attempted to keep in step with vacillating Moscow doctrine.

By the late thirties, before the signing of the Hitler-Stalin non-agression pact, the young Reds sponsored a coalition movement within the ASU, bringing it toward outright alignment with the administration of President Roosevelt. Socialists in the union, rebelling at such a position, withdrew, so that by 1938 the ASU was representative of the Left in name only. As it had in the early days of the First World War, the issue of preparedness and war against the Fascist states again caused splits within the radical student population. When the war came, with millions of men going to two theaters of conflict, campus politics was all but wiped out as the nation mobilized to meet the demands of its developing war psychology. Since then, and until recently, there has been little radical activity. And except for a token movement in support of communism and then Henry Wallace's campaign (Progressive Party candidate in 1948) the silence of radicals is the first dozen years of the Cold War was, to use a cliche, rather deafening. The exact reason for quiet during those years is difficult to ascertain. Certainly, the fear Senator Joseph McCarthy promoted (and which many others employed), reached every corner of American life, including the life of colleges meeting the burden of home-from-the-war veterans—veterans who had to resume roles and find a place in a nation touchy and tense. The ethic of these years embodied a belief, cynical though it was, that life was tough enough without special political troublemaking; that it was significant enough for the young man to cut himself a niche in the world in which he could reside comfortably and securely and moderately. But a spark would fly in the sixties, ignited by the tension of a two-decade Cold War and the failure of many Americans to realize the hypocrisies inherent in the practice of welfare capitalism.

When a newspaper headline blares "War Protesters Tramp Streets Across Nation" it is calling the public's attention to one of the most expressive, most telling forms of what's happening throughout the nation. This does not mean that anyone with an interest so inclined, shows it in such a decisively open way. The candor implicit in the modern social protest movement is often absent in usual confrontations between those outside and those inside the reigning order. For this reason so much of America's present kaleidoscope of change is misunderstood, feared, regretted, and labeled deviant. And it is evident that lines of communication between society's political fringe and society's controlling core have degenerated into a frazzled cable that distorts and cuts messages going in both directions. Paradoxically, although there exists a standard fascination with the outsider ("isn't he a cute idealist"), there also exists a revulsion toward the objections he makes and political dissent is often greeted with "what's he beefing about, he never had it so good."

The telling characteristics of the New Left are not many, nor are they especially clear. But among them is a striking disruption from the Establishment's way of doing things. (Most will even balk when asked to submit to conventional society's demand to define terms, such as "Establishment.")

This might be caused by frustration in trying to get things changed by the rules, or by an expressly stated desire to extend the conflict beyond a limited range—to get it out in the open where a larger public can be drawn in and politically felt. Whether it is frustration or involvement with conflict, their feeling is that the Establishment won't bend unless they make it feel pressure.

A second feature is an ambivalent issue-transcending righteousness that provides justification for all types of social protest. America has often been beset by fetishes of a moral nature and righteous indignations and this is a similarity with the past. But America has made a god of the pragmatic way of life and this is what those who protest disdain. These individuals won't respond to the twentieth century's clarion call for an end to ideology. Instead, they demand controversy over ideologies—even over the point of their dismissal as a political fact of life—and not an ending of discussion about them. Nobody is declaring that righteousness is bad; however, there is a declaration that social ills demand attention, not fogged glasses, and that attention reaps reward when accompanied by the moral fervor of those, as the saying goes, "who feel deeply."

Not all the revolutionary town criers in present America are young, nor are they ideologues in the sense that the radicals of the thirties were. It's been said several times that today's rebels are characterized by a non-ideological political commitment, a philosophy more akin to Camus than Marx, a commitment that leads to distrust of the State and distaste for those who run the State and the social institutions that rely on the State for their existence. They have a cause and they are not afraid to use a blowtorch to make their point—the picket, the sit-in, the mass parade.

But we have refrained from identifying these radicals as ideologists, because what's happening politically seems to be one of those rare, apolitical social movements. Examination of various groups and individuals of the Left reveals a certain amount of structure, a certain number of defined goals, at least a considerable degree of planning for the future, and a definite orientation that demands adherence from believers. Today's gospel is the Ideology of Concern and Action, hung together with diffuse notions of humanitarianism.

The political corner is significant in still another way. It is a stepping off point for many on the road to other happening scenes such as drugs, sex, or literature. A fact always in the mind of anyone who is a political organizer is that there is a constant flux in and out of political action groups, and this flux mirrors the changing feelings of efficacy or personal effectiveness on the part of the membership. Individual attitudes of powerlessness and meaninglessness prevail in all areas of the revolution taking place, but they become striking when one considers the strong, now weak, now strong flights of the modern rebel. It takes action and response to keep them going. It takes a society that feels the heartburn of Negro desires and expectation and a society that seems fretfully inept at relieving the indigestion by living up to its own standards. It takes a society that reminds the historian of the mass nationalism that precedes great wars—a nationalism that serves to reaffirm some insecure nation's identity rather than make a whole world safe for democracy.

It is reported that the New Left has a three-fold gripe and these complaints are behind everything they do in the way of social action, of movement and of protest. This generation's radicals do indeed focus on civil rights (voting and equal protection of the laws), peace (Vietnam and disarmament) and poverty (community aid, retraining, and basic education); but beyond this schedule of activities lies a duality that gives a great human meaning to these young people. They have a sparkling optimism about the future (except for those who've turned the corner of political ambivalence) and they possess a cynical mistrust of the

Establishment, or, as some have put it, "anyone over thirty who doesn't swing."

One of the factors that distinguishes the New Left from radical movements of the past is directly related to this cynicism about the Liberal Establishment and the way it runs society. For those politically inclined, the State is becoming a symbol of abject disillusionment. It symbolizes what "they" (the Liberal Establishment) failed to accomplish when they had their chance, and it is representative of a two-directional alienation in American culture: alienation of the body politic from the government and alienation of the government from those they rule. "Hope" is no longer personified by the State, and as centralization and bureaucratization slowly encroach on individuality, the New Left wonders whether the State can actually be a valuable tool in building more humane relationships in a mass society.

The sixties will weigh heavily in American history. Because of its civil rights movement, this era will be seen as the moment in time when equality and freedom, as philosophical precepts relating to man's position in terms of other men and the State, flowed together. As the moment when American civilization was presented with a fact of life —equality and freedom for all are *necessary* in a functioning and truly democratic system. The movement to recognize both as vital parts to man's very existence has been writ large in everything the New Left attempts. In fact, it is at the base of the hang-loose ethic, which though it evolves politically into anarchy, still demands that in human relations of any scale, the worth of the other shall not be reduced by withholding that which is rightfully his. No longer, says the Left, shall equality and freedom be found separate, or even contradictory. Both must exist together if we're to have a social system that caters to its members in a human fashion.

For those deeply concerned about the state of American society, with its inequalities, discrimination, subjugation, and noxious gratifications, a major question must be asked.

128

Historian Howard Zinn, in his book about the Student Nonviolent Coordinating Committee, poses the query as he wonders how commitment should be measured. "Is it the willingness to take a day out of life and sacrifice it to history, to plunge for one morning or one afternoon into the unknown, to engage in one solitary act of defiance against all the arrayed power of established society? Then tens of thousands of young people, mostly black, some white, have committed themselves these past four years, by the simple act of joining a demonstration." But it could be more. It could be "the willingness to wrench yourself out of your environment and begin anew, almost alone, in a social jungle which the most powerful forces in the nation have not dared to penetrate."

But bringing commitment to your effort is not distinguishing in and of itself, for devotion is anything but a stranger to political and social protest. History has known true believers throughout. Martyrs have come and gone and, certainly, more will appear in the future; but there are aspects of the New Left's beliefs and style that denote qualitative differences between today's radical commitment and those of the recent past. We have already mentioned one—the presence of an attitude that can be called rejectionism. Another difference has also been indicated, of lacking a structured, political ideology which would dialectically outline social ills and just as pointedly dictate *the* method of correction. If anything, the New Left has several hazy party lines, not one. In this respect, a faculty member's comment to a young assistant seems appropriate. This former radical of the thirties said, "You've got no ideology, no program." In his next breath he followed with the apparently contradictory statement, "why the hell are you so dogmatic?" But there does exist a dogmatic, often pedantic apoliticism among the numbers of this generation's committed. It's not labeled or identified by any party designation, nor even tagged by a particular theory. There are Marxists and neo-Marxists; Trotskyites and Leninists; Maoists and admirers of Castro; but those who can be referred to with even these presently mutated labels are a minority of the minority, and, strangely enough, they are frequently accused of being the moderating influence in many local action movements. "They're too concerned with the damn system as it is to really move," said a radical who favored a consistent policy of thumbing one's nose at the entire existing structure. "We've got to go outside to be truly effective. Unless we do that, and do it often, we'll become nothing but feed for the sows."

A purely statistical view of today's movement reveals another difference from the recent past. There is an intellectual elite (it must be called that regardless of how much the rebels detest use of such terms) that is larger in numbers and better educated in terms of years of schooling and degrees than any in the American past. These people no longer offer their ideas about policy and reform to traditional outlets, which for the last few decades in this country has usually been the Democratic Party. Faculty and student brain trusts are now so numerous that no one standing organization or established publication can possibly soak up their varied conceptions about society as it is and society as it should be. Because of this, new outlets have been developed in the journals both print and the organizations they've started. The publication of *Studies on the Left* in 1959 and *New University Thought* the next year marked the beginning of new wave leftist journalism to campuses, libraries, and homes across the country. The *New Republic, Nation,* and *Progressive* were supplemented and then replaced as the New Left's radical development took shape.

Other non-political factors mark distinctions between today's rebels and those of our nation's past. Not only are they intelligent and mature for their years (they can get good grades and they can responsibly carry out obligations despite the fact that youth today—the ones we're talking about—supposedly can't do either), but they remain detached from adult supervision and heavy-handed guidance. These aren't the youth leagues of another generation's Communists and Socialists, they are students on their own, supporting their own movement with their own fired-up manpower, and shaping as clearly as possible what they want as their particular destiny.

Yet this assumption of independence has its side effects on youthful radicalism. Potential for disillusionment has a habit of increasing in proportion to the intensity of an individual's commitment to a general ideal or a specific program. Coalitions of adults and youths are not sharing all the radical efforts and it seems harder for the young rebels to accept the fact that winning their point usually involves a tremendous compromise and even an emasculation of earlier dreams. Having drawn attention to themselves by their actions, the New Left must learn to live with a quickly dissipating influence on governmental policy. Moving in on a vacuum of political discussion during the early sixties, young people are now used to being listened to and paid attention to. But with the introduction of more traditional and moderate influences into political debate (e.g. the Senate Foreign Relations Committee hearings on Vietnam) their voice gets shunted aside, their idyllic innocence gets obscured, they have difficulty getting coverage for their views and statements, and the potential for disillusionment increases phenomenally.

Much has already been written about organizational looseness on the New Left, a fact of life that can contribute to confusion and chaos, but which can also lead to the spirit and camaraderie of beautifully functioning organizations. The Free Speech Movement, for example, is seen by many on the Left as the perfection in one setting of organizational efficiency and individual freedom. The emphasis on ideal democracy within much of the Left is stronger today than in the past, but all too often meetings have a stark resemblance to a corporation's stockholder gathering —the people are there, but they don't have all that much say about future policies and long-term stances. Subservience of the group to the individual has become a general framework, though, for leftist organizations, and an accurate representation of this might be "I'm a guy who happens to be in SDS, not SDSer who happens to be a guy." The fluidity of memberships and participation this looseness fosters contributes to the high turnover rate of leftist organizations as well as the large number of overlapping group memberships. The children of the next generation will have parents, in greater numbers than ever before, who went out and did something. This is a further point, the New Left notes, the Establishment should consider now while it is planning our future.

Commitment, non-ideology, a quizzical look at the role of the State, independent intellectual agility and promotion lead directly to another fact about today's radicals. They have, are, and will continue to perfect, the revolutionary style and spirit of social action. The divisions within the Left fall here, not on the strategy and tactics of operations, but on the overall style. The splits fall not on the form but on the content—the approaches toward the purpose of radical politics, its relationship to the ruling system, and the role of radicals in constructing a spiritual community. Whether the arguments can be resolved, given their top-flight sophistication about action and ideas, is the big problem for the future. Will the Left break up because one camp believes a real system can't be precisely defined (therefore permitting coalitions with labor unions and government agencies), and the other faction thinking a system can be discerned and should be avoided to prevent contamination? Will the Left dissolve into bickering and ineffectual proclamations, reverting to arguments over strategy and following the well-worn path of earlier radical movements? Or, will the New Left stay bound to common interest and revolutionary purpose?

Traced to at least four important happenings during the years surrounding its rise, the foundations of the New Left are first seen in the progress of the civil rights movement from the moment of Martin Luther King's participation in the Montgomery bus boycott in the fifties. Applying techniques of civil disobedience and of earlier labor struggles in this nation, then adding their own especially suited tactics, the rights movement blossomed by the beginning of the sixties. The real force behind the drive for full equality became by 1960 and 1961, and is to this day, its students. (Here as elsewhere in this report, "students" should not be considered only as those enrolled in colleges, rather the word should apply to actively participating youths in general.) Whether they are Negroes from segregated colleges in the South sitting-in at lunch counters, or whites (along, again, with Negroes) moving to the South for direct action after months of work in their home territory, the civil rights struggle has come to rely on students for brains and manpower, success in the past, and achievement in the future.

There was little surprise within the movement in the summer of 1966 when the opposition cried out at the use of the expression "black power." For many, this adoption of a public race consciousness was the capstone on student led radicalism, despite the fact that the term only attempts to promote political, social, and economical advancements for a specific minority group. The Student Nonviolent Coordinating Committee (SNCC), founded in the South in 1960, had been loud and explicit many times before it started the black power business. Now with its members and supporters laying it right on the line (and exposing breaches in the supposedly solid civil rights field) they were no longer just "big mouthed kids with good intentions," but became "bigoted brats," though they were clearly advocating the traditional American political policy of bloc voting. The civil rights movement, the spark that got the whole radical show on the road, is today torn over a question that could rip assunder the entire New Left. How far along the line can we really work within the Establishment without actually trying to take over the operations ourselves? Can we stay with the system, getting handouts now and then, and still manage to secure radical change in America?

The resurrection of a concerted peace movement was a second factor in the development of the New Left. Formed in 1960, the Student Peace Union was modeled after the British C.N.D., including use of the same symbol to fight for disarmament and an end to war. Though the SPU broke up in the several months following the signing of the nuclear test-ban treaty, many of its members soon joined what is this moment's peace effort—reflections on United States' military involvement in Vietnam and American foreign policy in general. The peace movement became the second front of the New Left and a collage of groups sprung up to meet the test, some remnants of older outfits, others a collection of rebels wanting completely independent organizations. Largest of these groups is the National Coordinating Committee to End the War in Vietnam, itself a confederation of nationwide anti-war groups. Headquartered in Madison, Wisconsin, and responsible for directing (at this writing) three International Days of Protest, the Committee includes in its structure, Berkeley's Vietnam Day Committee, an organization regarded in the popular mind—perhaps not without good reason—as the most notorious of the protesting youth groups.

Out of this new peace movement has come the famed teach-in, a lengthy discussion by "experts" about a specific problem (*e.g.* Vietnam). Having its first big show at the University of Michigan's national teach-in during spring,

1965, this method of protest (and that is what the teach-in has become) pays tribute to the ongoing spirit of the New Left. "Too much talk, too much theory, not enough action and fact," reads the charge against the Left of the past and today's Liberals. The teach-in is a concession to the standard appeal for reasonable discussion, but that's as far from the streets and byways the New Left is willing to travel.

If civil rights and peace form the substantive base of the New Left, Fidel Castro and John F. Kennedy are its metaphysical supports—both infused the atmosphere with a spirit of movement and change, key words in Leftist dialect. Where Castro moved those already on the Left, it was Kennedy who moved many to the New Left with the dynamism of social concern attributed to him and his administration. The cover declaration of the Students for a Democratic Society's Port Huron statement portrays the sense of purpose and urgency drawn from these philosophical groundings. . . . " . . .We seek the establishment of a democracy of individual participation governed by two central aims: that the individual share in those social decisions determining the quality and direction of his life; that society be organized to encourage independence in men and provide the media for their common participation." SDS is but one of several groups on the left of America's political continuum. They might be called left-wing socialists in any other nation, but in this country they and their actions are radical, though the ideals they act in support of may seem like, and indeed are, the misplaced values for two hundred years of Americans.

If there is any one moment that is the glory of the New Left, it must be that night in December, 1964, when policemen dragged several hundred live bodies from the Berkeley campus of the University of California. For many, the Sproul Hall sit-in is synonymous with "The Day"—the day radicals come of age, brought a university to a virtual chaotic standstill and managed to inspire educational and

*135*

political change that has yet to stop. To students and former students across the country, the Free Speech Movement lived in the very image of the young generation's aspirations—it was a community, shaped in response to conflict, searching for the path that leads to freedom and learning in modern society. Goodman has stated that the exploited in our society are the college and high school students force-fed into higher education; middle-class individuals who by press and circumstance are herded through the doors of academia, given the choice of getting a degree or withering away. Representing the "revolt of the slaves" are the Free Speech Movement and the related uprisings that have scored the educational plain in the past two years at such schools as St. Johns, Yale, Chicago, and Rutgers. As many administrators have already observed, today's active, if affluent, college student is not arguing solely about conditions. He doesn't really *hate* the two-car garage, his father's income, or a relative's expense-paid trip here and there across the continent. He's asking questions, thinking about proper perspectives, talking about meanings and espousing the need for change.

The New Left resides amidst the spirit of a world gone mad. Most won't cloud their thoughts with weighty pronouncements about winning battles and losing wars because every day can seem crucial for achieving the goal in mind. It is not too difficult for these people to sense that this planet could very easily be blown to bits by the intolerant and irrational few that, so they believe, control the strings over the puppet masses. A fear and a growing disillusionment with about everybody but themselves lies beneath almost all of this decade's radical activity. "They've blown it, baby, and they won't admit it, so it's up to us to maintain a cool for the future," commented a rebel during a picket line interview a few years ago in Baltimore.

We can't answer the question whether or not the older generation has really flunked the test of life in this modern and devastating era. What is significant is that those who protest, who march, who teach and demand, really do believe that's the way it is. They see as the irony of a lifetime (or, for the cynic, as the end of life itself) the point that even though yesterday's generation flunked out of class, they now own the school, have lowered the standards below their own failing point, and continue to sink lower and lower into the mire of their own ineffectiveness. It does not matter to these people, for example, that the blackmark of McCarthyism was almost completely eradicated from the formal life of American politics (for it still lives on informally), but it does matter that it could have arisen at all. Things like McCarthy's crusade during the early fifties, Eisenhower's technique of non-government, the spread of a radical right, an ostrich-in-the-sand Liberal Establishment are not warts, nor mutations, but actually symptoms of the whole body's disease. These radicals are looking for cures to aid a political, economic, and social order now in a terminal state. One of the small number of radicals to be found at most schools, who happened to be a regular reader of the *Wall Street Journal* ("to keep up with the enemy"), said with a sickness in his voice, less than two years ago, "Look, man, Holy Christ, General Motors made a net profit of more than a billion dollars this year. It's almost impossible to think of all that money . . . . in their hands . . . . when you know, you just know what good it could actually do."

Previously, we wondered whether what's happening to large portions of our younger generation is a reflection of revolt against the authority of elders or whether it is a general symptom of a sickly society—the revolution or the rotten apple. Disaffection and rejection seem to be the key words, and alienation the crucial concept. Regardless of whether the happener has been pushed outside, he soon comes to actively question dominant themes of this society and his surrounding culture. For this reason, the movement in the sixties is far from over. And it would not surprise the authors if in the next few years a silent transformation will infect American radicalism with again a new perspective, a view that will claim activity as fruitless and the total system as something corrupt and unsalvageable. Indeed, this has already happened to some young people. This would be a most radical position for it accepts not only rejection of the going order, but presupposes that the system doesn't even merit the consideration required in outright, active rebellion. Some would call this position apathy, but actually it would be an utmost in extremism. These people would be more than disinterested; they would be totally disenchanted and disillusioned with a political order that openly admits its use of lies, deception and corruption. Despite the fact that a doctrine of withdrawal would be held by the smallest of minorities, in absolute figures, it does pose an issue for the rulers of the Great Society, a society in which all men, it is dreamed, will be part and parcel of organizing and maintaining man's most noble achievement.

At the present time, the New Left will go where it wants to. It will progress with the creative power it can muster, gradually gaining adherents to its causes, or it will pass in good time as so many other radical movements have done. But it doesn't seem that death is a reasonable prophecy for the future of American radicalism. Instead, it seems to be one of the forerunners of widespread social and ethical change in the American mind. Perhaps it was Goodman who struck the proper note about the politics of political and cultural rebellion when he observed that this could be one of the few student revolutions in man's history that had meaning beyond its peer group. A revolution that turned the rest of the population onto its causes, goals and philosophy of life, leaving its imprint for future generations to judge, and, hopefully improve upon.

## 8 / the education bag

How many college administrators sigh for bygone days of the old-fashioned snake dance victory parade, the beer blast, and the panty raid? There are no more student princes or gentlemen's flats, and the cloistered, tree-lined buildings and walks have given way to the more functional layouts needed to handle new crowds. Polished wood is being replaced by glass and concrete block, and swarms of students now overflow the rooms and lawns like bright locusts descending upon a sleepy green field.

Recently, a faculty member with the security of tenure, at a large midwestern university, instituted a program designed to get more out of his students and at the same time give them more of an education. For the professor, education was a personal thing, which should involve going outside the lecture hall (in this case, packed with 450 students) and meeting the students head-on; giving them a feeling of actual, active participation in the learning process. After setting up a control group, he gave personal attention to two score students following the release of mid-semester grades. He deliberately chose sudents who had not done better than average ("C") work in an attempt to verify his long held assumption that if, somehow, we could get to the passive student at the large school, that student's productivity in terms of his grade would vastly improve. Indeed, this assumption was verified. All but a few of the youths selected showed marked improvement on a second mid-semester test as well as on the final course examination.

At another institution, a faculty member called upon his students to participate in a survey he was conducting. Their interviewing, he whimsically noted, would help him score points in the school's "publish or perish" game that was the real, if unpublicized and publicly denied, basis of faculty advancement and security. His students laughed at his utterances, all too aware that both they and their teacher were captive members of the giant administered bureaucracy that is modern American education.

The field of education is currently embroiled in a series of hot debates, of ringing indictments, and righteous re-buttals, of investigating committees and mounting student and teacher complaints. The variety of factions seem to agree on only one point—that whatever action is now being taken to correct the "faults" is still haphazard, groping, and sadly ineffectual. Most of those involved in education, in-cluding the happeners, are in the stage of mass contempla-tion, but increasing numbers are going the routes of mass action and mass withdrawal. Renovation is the hope of most factions and the problem of broadening and enriching educational opportunities is now the concern of faculty committees, students, and even some administrators.

From nursery school through the postgraduate institute, American schooling is a mirror reflection of general trends in our mass society. Its growth has become increasingly centralized and though we still don't have a master federal program of education, our schools have become bureauc-racies, more and more interlocked with governmental-industrial-military bureaucracies, and more and more in-distinguishable from them. The dispensation of rewards in this system—and what must be done to earn the rewards—also reflect our growing standardization. Publicly financed elementary, high, and university schools have grown so much during the last half-century that few students today attend private institutions and education has become a major item in the budgets of local, state, and national governments. And massive public education has brought with it systematized approaches in teaching and in sorting and culling students. For the five or six year old child, this is "where it's at" during the next eleven or twelve years of his life. He is bombarded with tests and interviews that, from the start, try to categorize and departmentalize his learning ability, and for the rest of his life, he will be a captive of whatever record he earns. Variety and possibility for personal growth are too often ignored, as school systems strive to meet society's demand that the direction and potential of all its incoming participants be measured.

The breath of public education is by no means confined to the first twelve years of school. Increasingly, higher education, especially in the Midwest and the West, has come under the influence of mass, centralized systematization. And the process of sorting, categorizing, and departmentalizing which started in kindergarten and first grade is continued—but only for those who have been slotted for a college education. Indictments of education in the past decade have focused on this trend: young people are needed to meet the demands of the social order and the system in turn has devised methods for insuring its continuance, often neglecting the needs and potential of the individual student.

As has been frequently shown, education has a precise role in today's society. It is the means for maintaining the cultural, social, and political dominance of middle-class values. Illogical though it may be, public high school students in south central Los Angeles (predominantly Negro) are subjected to the same curriculum as those in West Los Angeles (predominantly white). The fact that the actual participants in the school system—the students—may be worlds apart is rarely recognized, as cities, counties, and states set up standards for education's operation. It is a matter of empirical fact, that large numbers of students—at all levels—are, to borrow Heinlein's phrase, "strangers in a strange land." Education today looks not from society to the individual, but from the individual to society. Where is his place? What can we do with him? But these are questions antithetical to the essence of the learning process which asks the student to wonder, "what should I do with my society?" The fact that children of the permanently unemployed, the racial minorities, and the disenfranchised in general are not part of the total system does not make this question any less important. Directing these people to conform to a mold—as do the vast majority of those already in the middle-class—will benefit neither them nor society in the long run. It is the problem of American education to recognize distinctions in values and aspirations, and even to promote these distinctions, for it is education and the learning process that supposedly serves as society's constant critic through its findings and admonitions.

Because society demands compulsory school education and also condemns other forms of learning such as just "bumming around," students today feel compelled to go along, to contribute in a manner already decided, and to become part of the larger order once they have completed the required tasks. But what is so significant in the formal education process that permits only those with high school or college degrees to acquire certain occupations after graduation? What is the reasonableness of a doctrine that permits someone with a bachelor of arts parchment something that someone fifteen units short of a degree cannot attain?

Sociologist Edgar Friedenberg has commented in an essay, "We are back, then, to the point that the schools are an integral part of the system by which the dominant social and economic institutions of our society staff themselves and propagate their values. What is new to us is the *totality* of the process. Society no longer brooks any alternative to school attendance; the schools no longer permit their students much voice or choice about what kind of persons they shall be encouraged to become." Paraphrasing Paul Goodman, today's middle-class children are educational slaves. If the disenfranchised in our society are bludgeoned into completing high school, the middle-class youth is pushed towards the college education. For many, this is viewed as merely extending the same evil, albeit the middle-class student resides on a higher level.

American education has become not solely a tool for the expression and promotion of factual learning, but also a powerful socializing element within the culture. As an instrument of society's dominant interests, regardless of how vaguely their values can be defined, the American school system functions on three intersecting planes. It is first a "pressure cooker" that keeps rumblings under control by giving young people a respectable position in society. The student becomes occupied with getting through his years in school; adjusting to the demand that an education be completed; and accepting the fact that his right to disagree and to advocate change comes with a diploma and not before. One of the important things currently happening in American education is the recognition that the "pressure cooker" has too tight a lid, that the small amount of exhaust permitted is *too* small in terms of personal dignity and respect. Many students are complaining today even if their proposals for change are limited, and the "pressure cooker" role of education is in danger.

In high schools and colleges and graduate schools, education is also a "personnel officer." There are numerous school boards around the nation which institutionally provide for two distinct teaching programs. The first is vocational education in which the student (who by benefit of testing and attrition has been placed in this category) is trained to assume certain needed roles in society. Manual training programs, as they are sometimes called, provide our carpenters, our electricians, and other skilled craftsmen. Such training is often quite good and enables its graduates to make a decent wage, although they must face the growing spectre of job obsolescence.

The unskilled workers in society are also funneled into their position through the "placement" influence of the educational process. As the system casts them aside, or as they realize the fact that there is not a ready-made place for them within the school order (as there is for the middle-class youth), the disenfranchised youths are literally pushed beyond the realm of acceptable occupational aspirations. For those that don't have a place or a desire within the overriding American ethic, the school systems hold little promise—unless the individual manages by fair deed or foul to get "in" and "with it."

The "personnel officer" function is especially applied during the college and post-graduate years. By going to college, by getting that prized degree, the student can assume his place as a participating member of the American system. This is the carrot on the end of the stick. Even if he does not eventually assume a position of influence or control, the college educated individual, by virtue of education's magic-wand, is at least not automatically denied such possibilities. Colleges provide our nation's managers, the professional technicians, and the owners of the corporate state. Beyond this, they also provide the updating of knowledge and fact required to keep the system running smoothly forward. Large numbers of students are today realizing that a college education should have as its motto "damned if you do and damned if you don't." Exploring the alternatives preoccupies many at this moment, but it is questionable just how much can be done given the expressed demands of society upon its educational order. It is problematic whether or not our nation's giant corporations—who foot the tax bill for large segments of higher education (though the cost is passed on to their customers)

—would really consent if college faculties dictated a removal of the corporation from the campus. A removal—from the visiting recruiter during one's senior year to the research grant—that would cut off easy access to both personnel and knowledge.

Aside from roles already mentioned, the college is also a "measuring cup." College training is today's first significant measure of status and achievement for young adults. Such measures establish one's starting place for future social and economic competitions.

One can't help but wonder, whether or not any or all of these roles can be eliminated from the education atmosphere. We already have a going system, that, undeniably, fulfills many of the desires our society expresses. It is just as true that large numbers of students readily accept, if not wholly approve, the way things are. Battles over the future of education must meet the challenge posed by those who have "learned the art of surrender," for it is these young people who are going along with the molding process, and who even look forward to the day when the drummed-in faith fills their cup with social blessings.

Any educational revolution today will have import only if it can strike at the ruling ethic in the American learning system—the ideology of democratic centralism. Modern education is big business. One need only look at the budgets of our larger institutions and school systems. At the university level, a few colleges soak up the largest percentage of research monies, which in turn support numerous and varied activities—usually unrelated to teaching in any form whatsoever, and, many claim, unrelated to any real scientific or scholarly achievement as well. Those schools already in this category and those aspiring to financial solvency (and increasing independence from trustees and legislatures) have adopted the efficient mechanism of democratic centralism in order to achieve the goal with a minimum of fuss or factionalism. Democratic centralism is a concept applicable to many institutions in industrial societies. It applies to nations and corporations, as well as school systems. Its economic counterpart appears to be the managerial bureaucracy, the means of designating expenditures, promotions, and intraorganizational relationships. If democratic centralism is the theoretical viewpoint, managerial bureaucracy is the occupational (or, if you will, the institutional) fact of life.

There are four aspects to the official theory. First, a requirement that there be regular, planned "elections" which provide periodic review of those in control of a particular system. This gives representation to various and sometimes conflicting elements and implies the notion that differences can be legitimately, if not congenially, resolved. Second, the publication and dissemination of reports and conclusions and policies, thereby permitting the participants an overview of the way the program is functioning. This embodies the theory that a democratic process, at any level, needs informed citizens for its growth, continuance, and inspirational allegiance. Third, the principle of adherence to stated and approved policies, involving the subjugation of minority positions to declarations of the majority. And, fourth, the absolute binding nature of higher level decisions over lower level dispositions. Thus, theoretically, we have an elected chief (or group of leaders) who, however, are the captains of their own ship. Points one and two pay tribute to ideals of democracy; three and four to the efficiency of the centralist model.

Democratic centralism, and the contingent managerial bureaucracy, are probably the most "efficient" procedures ever devised by man for handling complex far-flung organizations with large memberships and this is why they have spread throughout modern societies. However, they combine to stifle opposition and dynamism, not just in national governments, but wherever it is adopted as a ruling manner of administration. For better or worse the presence of

146

such systems is grounded in the industrial nature of much of the modern world. Centralized, bureaucratic, and heirarchical, these organizations commonly offer tributes of legitimized democracy and self-rule. Election and succession in these systems occurs through cooptation. Those higher up nominate, appoint, or "elect" those who will follow in their paths. Sometimes, to placate rising opposition, and again submitting to a vague democratic ideal of proper conduct, conflicting factions are given specific roles within the ruling order. But it is not a situation where vacuums are filled; rather it is one in which those in control rarely permit a vacuum to exist. Because involvement in such structures entails acceptance (if not absolute adherence) of a certain value system, and the meanings congruent with those beliefs, rebels appear infrequently and are looked upon askance. The institutionalized ideologies of the modern world, extending from the nation-state to smaller social structures, are pretty much closed systems, accepting recruitment of only those who meet the qualifications, dismissing with a flick of the wrist those who don't profess the same commitment.

Applying these concepts to American higher education, as well as other forms of instruction in this country, it is obvious that conflicting values will make themselves evident and that it is the problem of the educational system to remain free from the restraint of finance and at the same time fulfill its age old commitment to a measure of academic freedom and social criticism. The reconciliation of financial need with a free system has brought with it educational concessions. Aside from the abandonment of teaching as a primary criterion and value in higher education, there are elements which pay a dubious homage to the struggle for social existence and acceptance. Professional schools permit the larger society's professionals to impose restrictions on the number of students they train. Testing and grading have become a means of student placement, rather than part of the learning process which supposedly reaps reward when mistakes are pointed out amidst an environment of constructive criticism. Credits and requirements have been established across the board, permitting the society (and the corporation) the privilege of judgment and condemnation. Universities are already toward the point long ago reached by public education during the first twelve years of schooling. Higher education is fast succumbing to the necessities of survival in the welfare corporate state. More and more, the college function of developing the moral and intellectual side of its students is being cast aside in favor of providing a service center for the larger society.

None of the instruments of educational submission are as anti-scholastic as the growth of the modern administration. Goodman has this to say on what often resembles a formidable monolithic obstacle in the achievement of a personal learning experience: ". . . there is a small army of administrators who do not teach and with whom students and faculty communicate on a formal and rarely pleasant basis. It is here that we must look most carefully if we are to understand why the growing complaints against the colleges have made so little dent. . . The effect of strong administration is to weaken the college by keeping the students out of contact with the teachers; the teachers out of contact with each other; and both away from troublesome or embarrassing controversy with the world."

College administrations, often fighting for their institution's social survival, must insure smooth waters as they go after grants and legislative benefits. The attempt to keep conflict at a minimum, the constant efforts that converge toward reducing faculty and student assertiveness within the university and outside communities, serve only to standardize education, minimizing disagreement in favor of the Grand Consensus.

For a growing number of students, school is seen as something of a drag. The idea of education is more or less accepted, but *becoming* educated is distinguished from going to school, and most high school and college instructors are regarded as hopelessly square and out of touch with the pulse of the times. A graduate student at an Eastern University complained that "the damn faculty is more interested in their authoritative sources and departmental petty gossip than our education. It becomes a matter of learning to live with it while sometimes striking out on your own."

On the one hand students are dependent upon their teachers for the credentials which are more and more the necessary minimum for entering almost any echelon of the adult world. And on the other hand they don't respect the competence or wisdom (as opposed to knowledge) of their instructors. When taken together, the result of these two factors is that students insulate themselves from most of their teachers; they behave toward them in ritualistic ways calculated to enhance or at least not damage their chances of making it in the "school game"; and they feel few qualms about using almost any means of doing so. They often don't feel guilty about cheating on tests, taking cram shortcuts, handing in one another's papers year after year. (The senior author reviewed a paper on the Black Muslims that had been submitted in eleven different courses. It was a good paper, too.) One loses no prestige among fellow students by occasionally using such methods. But there is a good deal of wistful talk among students about how swinging education could be—if it were different. Meanwhile, since they feel they are treated as impersonal IBM cards, they reciprocate by giving little allegiance back.

One leading administrator stated, "I don't believe we're inhuman," but, he along with thousands of accredited educators is also aware that the developed system does not match the ideal. It is difficult for the contemporary college person to realize that there should be more to higher education than grade-point averages, finals, prelims, and papers. The scholastic life and the norms that support the widespread current situation permit only rare excursions into the pure novelty of fresh and invigorating ideas, and when the trip is sometimes made it seems to last for too short a time. Getting through college, whether large or small, is almost never any trouble for the student willing to learn and apply the "rules of the game." The empty seats in many of America's colleges attest to the fact that for any young person there is a place somewhere. Course requirements vary along with the institution's status and admission requirements, but for the young man or woman just out of high school finding a college should not be a tremendously difficult task—though finding one that fits his self-conception and financial capabilities is an entirely different matter.

Most of the really decent education occurs at the periphery of the formal educational system although special programs are shown off to the public in much the same way that the plush admissions lounge of otherwise scurvy state mental hospitals are displayed for journalists and relatives. The education which seems most valuable to the students and which probably proves most useful in their subsequent lives are either the "showcase" programs such as honors and tutorial courses, which reach only a tiny fraction of the enrolled students, or, ironically, they are the low prestige and understaffed curricula such as home economics, craft courses, or the more esoteric electives in the humanities. The average student—in high school as well as college —finds the average course just average; neither interesting nor useful in his life and life-style. For him, the rich multiplicity of learning and growing is reduced to the one dimension of getting grades.

Because of the general rise in the level of education and sophistication in our society, and because of the greater experience and "textbook" knowledge of today's youth as compared with the youth of former times, and because of the more direct and intense confrontations with the complex modern world as it now is, the youth of today are surging forward. Although inevitably innocent of many of the realities of adult life because they have not experienced them, they are still precociously wise and they therefore resent the condescending and patronizing "now children, we're going to learn about the world" attitude of many teachers who don't really seem to know all that much about the world.

There is a large element of truth in this feeling, despite its youthful arrogance and the felt need to assert oneself. Beneath the flow of pedagogic words, students often dimly sense that they are in reality being required to learn last decade's or even last century's stereotypes. They want to have the real world which confronts them explained and they grow impatient with jargons and generalities which all too often tell them nothing; and not infrequently, their own images and intuitions, although less organized and articulated, are more valid. It is this drive for a sensitive attachment to a "real" world, a world that does not fit in with the previous generation's typology, that brings many to "direct action." A summer in the South, weekly visits on tutorial projects in America's ghettos, and assistance at state-supported penal and mental institutions represent a sampling of their efforts to learn about their modern environment. The learning is conveyed through experience, not textbooks or lectures. Large numbers of students have realized and lived in light of the belief that an education does not stop at the limits of the campus, that involvement with the "outside" is essential for one to be an intellectually aware individual.

Since the other avowed function of education, preparation for an avocation and role in life, is bound up with their diffidence toward the conventional adult world and the models it offers and enjoins them to adopt, they feel that the school is letting them down on both counts. They are less willing to accept the notion that their mentors know what is good for them and what is worthwhile and true.

*151*

On the basis of their own firsthand experiences with the impersonal mass production procedures which are coming more and more to dominate American education, they find the public statements of administrators, about educating "the whole person" and grooming them for a "creative life," sophomorically hypocritical. Particularly at the university level, they discover that most of their professors are relatively indifferent to teaching them or talking with them. The professors defend themselves by pointing out that teaching is utterly irrelevant to the fortunes of their own careers and, in fact, is detrimental. Paradoxically, teaching efforts may leave a concerned faculty man far behind the field in the "publish or perish" game; a game in which one can find nice correlations between the sheer *number* of books and articles published, but almost no correlation between teaching ability and salary or position.

Students today are generally tired of hearing excuses made for large segments of the educational industry. Their antagonisms are sometimes loud and immediately shocking, as with the Berkeley Free Speech Movment and similar efforts by young students at campuses across the country. More often, the drive for change is presented in piecemeal attempts to have students participate in the official governing structure of the university. Regretfully, these efforts seem to go nowhere, for, as with any large bureaucracy, control and policy-making develop from informal relationships and applications of power and authority. But opposition is expressed in a quiet, seditious form as well. Increasing numbers of students are exercising their spirit of inquiry by simply dropping out of school for a short time, transferring to hopefully more exciting and enriching colleges, and simply taking a longer period of time to graduate, thereby sampling courses that befit their broadening interests.

Of recent changes in American higher education, few seem to extend beyond stop-gap reforms in the administration of a student's scholastic career and rarely are these revisions made in the universities' assumed role *in loco parentis*. Most new programs are exemplified by honors and tutorial courses, special schools, abolishment of grades other than pass or fail, and general reduction by some schools of long structured student-faculty separation in and out of the classroom. But few of these programs could be called truly radical or revolutionary. And few get to the root of student disenchantment, which demands a more active role in their own educational advancement, a role free from petty, technical regulations and free from the suffocating impact of being one person out of several hundred in a large lecture room.

Now and then a college will introduce a plan that verges on being an educational earthquake, such as a requirement that students spend at least one semester every school year on the "outside," involved with jobs or problems in the workaday, live world beyond the ivy. But even these schools, their critics will claim, are still part of the system, if only in their acceptance of national standards of accreditation and financial credit ratings. What some current students are demanding, along with larger numbers of former students dissatisfied with the education they received, is a move completely outside the educational industry. For many, the instrument that fulfills this wish is the Free University.

Berkeley's Free University is one of several that have been formed in the past few years. Seeking to detach themselves from the muddy waters of conventional education, these schools—all privately financed—are managing to survive, and, in spots, thrive. This "campus" states that "The Free University is forged in response to an education both sterile and stultifying, an education which fragments our experience and distorts meaning, which confuses rather than encourages action, and which provides—behind the pretense of knowledge—escape from ourselves and the problems of our day.

"We protest by joining the emerging spirit of dissent.

This spirit grows from a sense of indignation and from an eagerness to clarify the alternatives and responsibilities of choice."

Who teaches the courses, now several score in number, at the various Free Universities in such places as New York, Los Angeles, and Berkeley? Usually, the teachers are those with the well-trained "sense of indignation." Present and past college instructors, discontented graduate students, activists, and specialists in certain fields, especially the arts and letters, are on the new schools' faculty.

Courses tend to be what a member of the "educational establishment" described as outlandish. Fundamental courses, naturally, are also offered, but usually reflect the fine radical toning of these schools. "Music," "Chinese," and the "Modern Theater" are there, but what really draws enrollment are titles such as "Studies in Civil Disobedience," "Perspectives on Violence," "Afro-American Music," "Reform in the American University," and "The Nature of Modern Man." Credit is not given in the sense that it can be applied toward a degree or toward a transfer to an established college. Payment is made simply for attending the lectures and participating in the program. The administration of these schools resigns itself to just handling the money and sweeping the buildings—nothing else; for, as the Berkeley school declares, these universities are seeking "to create a place where teacher and student, education and action can come together."

As the '60's wear on it becomes increasingly obvious that if we mean our talk about educating people to become richer, more creative human beings, then we must implement and expand those few programs that now do this to any extent. If we do not mean it, then we should cease our hypocrisy and recognize education as the giant babysitting institution it actually is and explicitly train the baby-sitters to be entertainers and custodians. One way or another, today's students would like an answer.

## 9 / the sounds of new music

Popular music has troubled Americans ever since the turn of the century when ragtime and jazz first began to evolve and be played in the off-limits sections of southern and eastern cities. From its inception, it was colored with some of the ill-repute of the peoples from which it sprang: the emancipated Negroes, the migrant workers and tramps, the back country and hill folk. And ever since the 1920's when Dixieland, jazz, and folk music first began to make their way into the mainstream of American society, many people have worried over the vulgarizing and immoralizing influence of the wild new music. They were viewed as pied-pipings to moral decay and the young who flocked to listen were scorned. A girl's reputation could be ruined just by being seen at places where the music was played.

In a sense, Dixieland, Negro rhythm and blues, folk music, and rock and roll are considered the illegitimate off-spring of the American arts, and consequently they have been shunned and shamed as much as loved and supported. These kinds of music—although indigenous to certain aspects of American culture—have always been morally suspect and their successes have never lost a taint of notoriety. In their purest forms, they have mostly existed around the fringes, and the musicians who played them were almost entirely outsiders by birth or by choice. When they did reach the mainstream channels of the society, it was almost always in a watered down form in which the guttural chords and the frank and penetrating lyrics were cleaned up and little of their original vitality survived. Many of the conventional artists, who the man in the street might think of as great jazz musicians or folk singers, were seen as temporizing mediocrities by the originators and their followers. To this day, for instance, a symbol of true involvement in some scenes is the ownership of an old, original "Leadbelly" album, uncut and recorded by a company, it seems, no one ever heard of.

These various musical traditions—suspect in themselves— form the basis of the new music which now virtually dominates the sales charts of single records and albums. The new music is a synthesis which has evolved from these traditions and which holds promise of continuing change. This synthesis has produced a kind of music that is, in many ways, new in both content and style. As with other influences (such as literature and fashion), the culture becomes reshaped and the receptivity within the general populace for the new music is probably of a higher order than that given by previous generations to *their* own brand of new music. Aside from the fact that in a short time over half of our population will be under twenty-one, there exist other allies within society. Children of the fifties who grew up with Presley, Little Richard, *et al.*, are now the young marrieds of the sixties and the strands of musical bondage are strong enough to keep them tuned to pop music stations on the radio; to keep them somewhat up to date with the newest sounds.

Yet, even with these quiet colleagues on their side, the practitioners of the new sounds evoke a strangely antagonistic opposition. It is not a fight against the music itself that arouses many today, but actually a feeling of conflict with those things to which the new music has become attached, especially drugs.

"Forceful" is one word often used to describe the new music. Whether loud or soft, upbeat or slow, a flat-picked guitar or a plucked sitar, it is more direct and candid in its sensuality or protest or chagrin. Even the songs depicting the confusions of the modern scene are more bold and candid and less evasive than the songs of even the most recent past. The lyrics are more realistic and sophisticated in the sense that the veils of obvious romantic distance are gone. Simple-minded jingles, while still around, are now being replaced by what not infrequently amounts to good poetry. The impact of the new fashion (it is still too soon to call it a permanent facet of American music) goes even to those groups and individuals caught within the whirl of its sounds and sales. That is, few young people will say that the Beatles, the Stones, or Dylan of 1963 are the same today. The sound is moving, dynamic, constantly adjusting to new revelations about the way things are.

As a constant companion to the happeners, the new music and its themes are a running commentary on their own changing lives. It often verbalizes and clarifies their own vague feelings and sometimes it provides directions about what to do. People dance, read, make love, turn on, chat, and walk along the beach to the background of its sounds. Teenagers wash dishes and talk on the phone while listening to it and almost no one can escape overhearing the music on jukeboxes, TV commercials, neighbors' phonographs, or the transistor radios of strolling youths.

The new musicians are the poets and troubadours of what's happening, and their work, as it is disseminated, becomes itself an active social force which shapes and spreads the themes it is describing. As chroniclers, these artists therefore are acting also as innovators and propagandists. As propagandists, they still cloak their thoughts behind frequently murky lyrics; words that are vague to censors or parents, but "in" with the listeners. For example, anyone who is really happening knows about "Mr. Tambourine Man's" relationship to the drug scene on the first spin of the disc. And it takes little native intelligence to catch the essence of what The Fugs are saying when they clamor "Kill for Peace." The music has become a chronicle of events and messages, with the latter approaching the esprit of past eras' revolutionary ballads. The words are different, and even though it's difficult to define the antagonists, the force of feeling and craving are all too clear.

There are many varieties of the new music and many aficionados would balk at even discussing them all together. Lumping them together aids us in discussing them, helps the student in comprehending their import for society, but it also diminishes what each style particularly offers. There are several distinguishable varieties of new jazz, a host of differing rock and roll sounds (variously called rock, folk rock, blue rock, jug rock, raga rock, and acid rock), a sprinkling of folk styles, and other sounds which do not exactly belong in any category and which give classification headaches to record store managers. But in most of the songs, the musical scholar can detect various admixtures of the influences mentioned earlier, and beneath the variety of style and phrasings runs the common theme of the new emerging ethos and style of life.

Taken as a whole, the new music embodies two messages. *"Come Swing With Me."* The crooning invitation to romance which was the mainstay of popular music during the thirties and forties and the essence of rock and roll in the fifties, has become more a direct invitation to dance the dance of life. This invitation—expressed in so many songs by the shout "c'mon"—is sometimes aimed specifically at a possible sex partner and is a thinly disguised proposition. But at least as often, it is a more diffuse exhortation for everyone to shuffle off their mantle of preoccupations and hangups and to come out where it's at. If you're uptight about things, well maybe you have good reasons, but when there's a whole world outside "a'grooving," why bother?

Let's go where the action is. The invitation to the dance of life is, in the last analysis, extended to everyone and it is as cordial and indiscriminate as the morning sun.

The second underlying theme is more disturbing: *"Myself a Stranger and Afraid in a World I Never Made."* This poignant feeling of being a stranger moving through an alien environment comes through sometimes as a bitter indictment of the Establishment which sharply focuses upon nowhere men, universal soldiers, sounds of silence, or desolation rows. At other points, the tunes are about more personal distresses; a yesterday, a solitary man, the magic missing in a supposed magic town, or the larger question, "where do you or I go?" In still other instances, the songs express an uncertain yet determined reassurance that the new world is the rightful homeland of the modern spirit, you can walk a cat named dog, have a groovy kind of love, seek elusive butterflies, and catch reflections in a crystal wind.

When combined, these themes infuse a powerful sense of seduction in the happening way of life, into the spirit if not the substance of the hang-loose ethic. The music proclaims that you, sir, are not alone in your overall disenchantment with the state of most human relationships, that you are one of "the seekers" searching for meaningful values without an always hovering parent or dollar sign.

It has been common in the past few years to speak of the alienation modern youths feel when they consider their historical relationship to current meanings and older customs. What the new music trumpets, as it blares from record stores, stereos, and dance halls, is not as much the presentation of the subjective awareness of an alienated individual as it is that person's call to others like him. It is a call predicated on the belief that folks have enough in common now to transcend the sluggish, nerve-stilling impact of generational alienation and to proceed up and onward to some better world.

The music reveals this transition and is changing at this very moment. Perhaps this idea that things not only can change, but should become new and different, is part of the underground diffusion of the hang-loose ethic. The bitterness and rancor of earlier years is absent more often than not. When pity is presented in today's music, it is most frequently an expression of remorse about something that has happened to the total scene or an admonition to the majority that the path they are on leads nowhere but along the cliff of destruction. Now and again, the songs declaim the "other" world, but more and more often they proclaim the need to go out there "to bring them all on in."

But that is not all there is to the new music. Outside of the sales charts and the big names and mass distribution and communications business that have grown up around them are two other facets of the musical scene. The first is the army of local amateur and semi-professional young musicians who play the new music live at teenage night spots, college action spots, weekend dances, and shopping center moonlight sales. Their competence varies from embarrassing to as good and original as anything you can purchase at your town's "music city." A very few of these will get some measure of fame, the fleeting fame of one successful record and one big season in most cases. In almost every instance they simply make music for themselves and others and pick up a bit of money to help keep them in instruments, pot, and candy bars. A few reach such notoriety in their own locales that they are favored over most of the big national names in the new and emerging music. San Francisco's "Jefferson Airplane" has long been known in that area, and at this writing they are gaining momentum on national charts. This group, and a few others like them on the West Coast, such as "The Seeds" and the "Mothers of Invention" in Los Angeles, manage to pick up more than pure pocket money, but, consistent with the ethic, they are usually content without cross-country glory and all the hassles inevitably bound up with fame.

*160*

Secondly, there is a smaller, less known world of musicians and fans which exists outside the sales charts and TV shows, but which is an important part of the happenings among the avant-garde and the action capitals. It helps to set the tone and color the lives of the more far out groups in much the same way that literary magazines influence the more commercially successful literary world. Here new styles are experimented with, worked out, and improved upon. Tastes in this fringe world of music, in which each little "group" often has its own balladeer, may run months or sometimes years ahead of what one hears on popular radio. Bob Dylan, for example, was appreciated by thousands of people and scores of other musicians, some of them eminent, before the average American knew his name as part of the breakfast table chatter. Other artists manage to have long careers with only the support of such an informal and underground audience, and they never make it in the bigtime music world—a fact of life which really pleases many of them. The life of such artists is often checkered and gruelling and they live like vagabonds floating on a sometimes smooth, sometimes choppy sea of existence. But there are usually friends to give them a drink or a joint, friends to offer them a bed, and even a girl with whom they can share it. If they are rootless, they are also getting to do what they want (and that's something, isn't it?).

Since youths buy most of the records and put most of the money in jukeboxes, their tastes have come to dominate the popular music world, although, with constantly recurring payola scandals, their philosophy is often ignored and even abused. Whether moralizers like it or no, this market is big business and catering to it is a multi-million dollar enterprise. Only on Broadway and in nightclub circles do older tastes hold sway, a fact that helps explain the emergence of the hippies' very own ballroom discotheques.

The rhythmic cacophony of notes that explodes at San Francisco's Fillmore Auditorium is not unmatched in America—in terms of both the performers and the audience.

Situated in an overwhelmingly Negro district in that city, the Friday and Saturday night concerts are attended by many from all races. Straight people go there, but they are obviously and splenderously in the minority and they tend to be happeners of a sort that simply groove on big sounds. Standing at the entrance is an enriching experience in that one human can see hundreds of others much like him, yet others who are often carved in a peculiarly individualistic way. This door standing exercise also reveals an extraordinary number of heads—marijuana, LSD, peyote, and so on —who have come specifically to experience. Indeed, the Fillmore is just that: an unforgettable journey into an arena not yet part of the American mainstream.

Proprietors of this establishment, and the owners of others in San Francisco and cities throughout the land, know how to cater to their select customers. Not only are the bands far better than those that usually play for high school or college dances, but the amplification is turned up to peak, enabling the listeners to immerse themselves in the music. Compounding this technical bombardment of sound are the musicians themselves who absolutely cover the microphones with their instruments and mouths. But music, even if it is good and loud, is not enough and it is the extra features that draw the Fillmore's exclusive clientele, that is, the drug happeners.

The first of the extra benefits, craved by even this unstructured union, is the accented darkness of the large ballroom. Punctuated by flashing rotating and changing lights, the walls and ceilings and floor provide ample physical and sensual delights for individuals who want to trip. One especially bright light, variously called a strobe or stroboscope, looks for all the world like burning magnesium foil, flips and turns and casts its powerful radiant glow over the entire crowd of happeners. If the eyes can be taken off this light and focused on others around the floor, they look strangely like actors from early motion pictures with a hurky-jerky appearance and a nonchalant unawareness of everything that is taking place around them.

The items provided for the benefit of these sensuous attenders goes on and on: a large block of seats just below and in front of the band platform provides space in which the individual can not only immerse himself in the music, but where he can really be drowned, if he so desires; a tableau above and behind the platform on which are cast movies without sound (such as a silent "King Kong") or liquid doodles in water color, thrown upon the wall by a distant projector; and the establishment keeps its cool, so to speak, by offering as refreshments such blase items as soda pop, near beer, gum, and candy. The Fillmore is a traveler's reality-fantasy revealing both the bond and the spirit of the happening world.

The lights that shine and spotlight, the lights that glow and reveal, are not the lights of an isolated instance in our culture. But neither is it in danger of being submerged amidst a mass produced glare of happening action spots around the nation. It is a demarcation line for most—a place in which people turn on to their own way of existence, and, for a growing number, it is a setting for realizing what could be termed America's redesigned style of life.

A survey of the record buying public's tastes indicates that except for a few distinct styles (such as hillbilly music, varieties of jug-band composition, and the Motown sound) the music of today goes from West to East, no longer traveling from New York's Tin Pan Alleys to the palm lined boulevards of Los Angeles or the hills of San Francisco. During the spring of 1966 for example, it was not uncommon to find big West Coast singers or groups virtually unknown in the East. It appears that the sounds, if not the musicians who make them, come from the shores of the Pacific, cascading across the continent to other scenes in other places. Ironic though it may be for the performers involved, it remains true that many of the current big figures in the new music found their first recognition amongst the record buying and concert attending public in the West. The majesty of these sounds draws musicians from all over the country in their effort to find a place in the sun; it also draws the attention of record manufacturers who realize the pace-setting nature of musical fashion that builds itself up under the flare of the California strobe.

The two main oppositions to the new music are that it is tasteless and that it is immoral. With its candor and irreverence, the music shocks many people, although some of the tamer tunes will set older toes to tapping. But to many people it is simply noise; humdrum tunes played badly, raucously and with little variation in style. Since they can find no musical merit to the sounds, and because they find the lyrics both "dirty" and "suggestive," they look about seeking the foundations of its popularity. The most common explanation is that the youth are sheep, following fads and being victimized by shady disc jockeys and managers. Others feel that the popularity is simply the result of the uneducated poor taste of youth and a reflection of the tendency towards outright barbarism, supposedly inherent in mass cultures. What we need, they claim, are more courses in musical appreciation, the presentation of "good" music on radio and television, and a self-servicing censorship body that would function for the record industry in much the same way as the movie industry's control board works to insure "cleaner" (and more insipid) films.

This view blends with the second charge that the music is vulgar in both a broad and narrow sense. Not only have the practitioners been branded on occasion with the stigma of sexual perversion, but some rightist groups have gone so far as to charge that the music is engineered and underwritten by the Communists as a means of subverting the morals of the country and as a hidden technique of brainwashing our populace. The evidence offered for such a conspiracy is that several people in the music world have been connected with such "Communist-front-groups" as the NAACP, the American Civil Liberties Union, SNCC, and, naturally, the University of California.

In a more moderate vein, many parents and others are concerned that the music may be too suggestive, downright sexually arousing for young people listening and dancing to the sounds and lyrics. Many who are real believers in the new music would rather not defend themselves against such positions for, it is their feeling, the notes and words are accurate presentations of their attitudes and emotions. As for those who claim that the music replaces intimate sexual relations by providing mass scenes of rhythmic orgasms, they respond, "look again . . . and, while you're at it, look at your own generation's music and the inhibitions it covered up."

These are happening times and the music of these times, more openly and blatantly than most other aspects of the happenings, leads the way to where it's at. With its ties to almost all the current scenes, the new music offers a substantive look at bits and pieces of the hang-loose ethic. It does not pretend to speak for everyone and his brother, but it does speak *to* them if they would just sit down and listen. The fact that this music so well portrays the temper of the generational change we have been discussing, is, itself, an open invitation.

# *glossary*

and, of course, by the time you read this it may well be out of date.


**acid**   lsd   see lsd

**backwards**   tranquilizers   any central nervous system depressant

**bad scene**   a situation likely to produce unpleasant experiences bum trips or distress or interpersonal trouble for those who become involved   more broadly anything which has unpleasant or disappointing qualities or consequences

**bag**   an interest or preoccupation or specific scene one is involved with   the bag image implies that one is enmeshed in something and thus less free to become involved with other things

**ball**   as a noun a good time a good scene a good trip especially but not necessarily a sexual one   as a verb to have a sexual experience particularly a very satisfying one   more broadly any especially good experience

**benny**   benzedrine   a central nervous system stimulant used to stay awake and to be more alert and by some to reach a mild high   physically habituating and deteriorating if used over a long period of time   the majority of users are depressed when they come down

**blood**   a negro   a neutral word which carries no taint of discrimination

*167*

**blow**    to perform well musically or verbally    to leave

**blow your mind**    to consciously experience stark amaze about a particular immediate happening or situation    fantastic astonishment often negative in one's subjective judgment

**bread**    money    more broadly maintenance expenses

**bug**    to annoy someone    to hang them up or create hassles for them

**bum trip**    a disquieting and unsettling subjective experience which leaves the person disturbed or shaken    more broadly any unsatisfactory activity or bad scene    also called a bummer

**bust**    an arrest    specifically a successful police action against those engaging in illicit activities especially drugs but also including abortions having sex or any activity which might lead to police harassment of some kind    the term implies that the ongoing behavior was interrupted and the participants are in some kind of official trouble

**cannabis**    botanical shorthand for two major variations of indian hemp    hashish    marijuana

**cat**    one who swings who is cool who is with it and where it's at    more broadly any male

**chick**    a girl who is sexually desirable whether she is straight or cool    more broadly any female

**connection**    source of illegal drugs    someone who is an intermediary contact and can aid with any agency which might be useful to the individual such as record business or police or abortionists    source of inside information    a sexual outlet    more broadly any relationship established between people

**contact**    connection into some particular scene or your reliable source of goods and services especially drugs

**contact high**    becoming high or turned on by simply coming into contact and interacting empathically with someone else who is up on psychedelics much as people do when others begin to yawn or laugh

**cool**   a general term for persons and things which are in tune with the modern scene        implies flair and finesse in moving within this scene and coping with contingencies and vicissitudes

**cop out**   give up        succumb to conventional pressures sell out to the establishment

**cope**   to effectively and competently handle ordinary tasks and encounters with straight society while under the influence of psychedelic drugs        to be able to handle contingencies even crises while tripping        usually the person must have had some previous experience with the drug before he can cope under any circumstances        ability to cope varies just as ordinary competence varies from person to person

**crash**   to fall asleep while using drugs or to come down hard and fast from a high or trip        for instance if a policeman approaches and questions you while you're up

**crazy**   a term of approval for someone or something which is really with it and trippy        implies approval of what the establishment would condemn that is being odd or different

**cut out**   leave        split        make it

**dealer**   a pusher        one who sells illegal drugs such as lsd marijuana pep pills and maybe anything else he can get his hands on        also called the man the connection

**dig**   to enjoy        appreciate        understand

**dope**   generally any drug        specifically marijuana or heroin

**drag**   something or someone that is debilitating        that turns one off and holds no promise of providing a meaningful or swinging experience

**dyke**   female homosexual        a lesbian

**fag**   a male homosexual        more broadly someone who is effete

**far out**   unusually high or extraordinarily bizarre        avante garde

**fix**   a shot of heroin or some other drug

**flip**   to be in any unusual state of being from far out enthusiasm to full blown psychosis       also to flip out or freak out

**forwards**   see speed

**freak**   generally a flipped out person       narrowly as a special type of head or frequent user of a certain drug such as an acid freak or a meth freak

**go**   to really get into the swing of something       to put in any kind of exceptional grooving performance       a shout of encouragement and support

**grass**   marijuana       see marijuana

**groovy**   swinging       with it       where it's at

**hallucinogenic drugs**   name given to psychedelic substances such as lsd and sacred mushrooms and peyote by those doctors psychiatrists and officials who believe that the effects of such chemicals is to produce hallucinations       in this view hotly contested by proponents of psychedelics the drugs produce a temporary state akin to the various kinds of mental disturbance       term hallucinogenic is seldom used by those who have actually taken the drugs themselves

**hang-up**   see hung-up

**happening**   an event particularly one that is likely to be a trip of some kind for the participants       implies excitement of something meaningful going on with a possibility of wonder and surprise

**hassle**   any unwelcome duty or intrusion on one's life or mental equilibrium as in don't hassle my mind

**head**   one who uses marijuana and or other drugs with enough frequency and involvement that they become an aspect of his life not just an occasional experience       the term implies a certain degree of involvement in and knowledge about drugs and the drug subculture       used as an identifying label among those who are and as a pejorative label among those who disparage drug users       as in acid head or pot head

**high**   to be exhilarated and psychologically turned on specifically by smoking marijuana or using other drugs       more generally being enlivened and aroused through any means such as music or fascinating conversation or a gripping movie

**hip**   in the know       aware of what's happening       experienced       with it

*170*

**hipster**    someone who is with it but maybe in more of a group consciousness and conforming sense

**hold**    to have marijuana or other illegal drugs on your person or close at hand

**horse**    heroin    h    hard stuff

**hung-up**    ensnared in a psychological or interpersonal problem and thus prevented from swinging

**hustle**    to bend effort to bring about some happening such as permission from an official or money from parents or the sexual surrender of a partner

**joint**    a marijuana cigarette    a place where things happen

**key**    about 2.2 pounds of any drug usually marijuana compressed into brick form    also spelled ki

**lid**    an ounce or so of marijuana and a standard size of marijuana transactions especially in the west    also called a can

**lsd**    lsd-25    lysergic acid diethylamide    a man made substance derived from the same mind-meddling materials that are found in rotten rye ergot    discovered accidentally in 1943 by a swiss chemist it remained an underground aspect of psychiatric therapy and cultural visionaries until the early sixties    sold by the dose in capsule or sugar cube or liquid form usually cut and is several hundred times stronger than most other psychedelics    no longer legally manufactured in this nation and its use is subject to increasing restrictions
it is definitely the most widely taken of the higher mind-manifesting chemicals

**marijuana**    a mild psychedelic made by curing the leaves and flowers of indian hemp    not physically habit forming although individuals may come to enjoy using it habitually as some people enjoy chewing gum or having water with their meals    intoxicant effects are not stupefying like alcohol and users do not lose control of themselves or do things they otherwise would not have done such as have sex or attack others

    effects vary to some extent but generally it heightens all of the senses and increases interpersonal sensitivity    according to some users it tends to intensify whatever mood the individual is in while others say it relaxes and uplifts them whatever their mood    presently outlawed in all states but its use is widespread as liquor was during prohibition    also called grass pot boo dope tea stuff mary-jane weed

**matchbox**   a small amount of marijuana usually five to eight joints      one fifth of a lid presuming to pass as one fourth of a lid      also called dime bag or nickel bag for ten and five dollar purchases in various locales

**meth**   methadrine      an especially strong stimulant taken in pill or crystal form and used habitually by a select group of persons known as meth freaks      reputation is questionable in happening circles

**out of sight**   so good that words and images fail to describe it

**police**   cop      nab      the heat      the man

**pot**   marijuana      see marijuana

**push**   to sell drugs or other illicit items and services more broadly to make any active attempt to manipulate your environment

**roach**   the butt of a marijuana cigarette

**scene**   the whole of a setting and the action occurring within it      includes both the physical setting and psychological mood and refers to the total organism/environment/activity      is analogous to the scene of a play with props staging actors and script

**score**   to obtain drugs or sex or generally to procure some concrete empirical goods or services or external recognition

**short**   a car

**spade**   a negro especially one who swings      a neutral term implying no discrimination

**speed**   amphetamines      any of the central nervous system stimulants such as dexedrine benzedrine or methadrine also called splash or chalk

**split**   to leave

**square**   a person or thing which is not in tune with or in the know about what is happening      implies being hidebound narrow and unimaginative in thought and feeling and behavior      used as a pejorative against someone or something which displays these characteristics

**stoned**     unusually high on lsd or marijuana     also loaded smashed ripped torn up

**straight**     in its narrow sense a person who isn't involved in or in the know about some scene the speaker is involved with such as drugs or protest movements or homosexuality more broadly it refers to a person or scene that is not connected with or very aware of the happening world like most parents professors and mass magazines     term is not necessarily negative in distinction to square which almost always is

**swing**     to become a spontaneous and effective participant in an ongoing thing such as sex or dancing or self expression also a way of describing someone who is usually with it

**teeny-bopper**     a teenage hipster

**toak**     to take a puff or hit on a marijuana cigarette

**trip**     an experience that carries the person outside his ordinary thoughts and feelings and perceptions and which involves him intensely in the unfolding immediate moment     usually involves heightened concentration and perceptiveness and a temporary loss of attention or concern with other things trips have an elusive subjective quality which can never be adequately communicated in words

**trip-out**     to become intensely involved in something so that one has the subjective sense of being carried away from ordinary concerns and carried along as a participant of some sort in whatever is happening     experience often seems bizarre because one perceives and feels differently almost as if for the first time so that the contrast with how one ordinarily perceives and feels is striking

**turn-off**     usually a passive verb meaning to be deadened or brought down to indifference and disinclination by something     to say that something turns you off is to say that it dispels whatever interest or enthusiasm you might have had

**turn on**     narrowly to smoke marijuana until one is high but more broadly and generally to be personally entranced and excited and moved by something from a sunset to a symphony to a pretty girl to a playing child to a psychedelic drug also means to come alive and carries the implication that conventional society creates people who are not very alive

**uncool**   person or thing connected in some way with the modern scene but displaying a gross lack of competence in swinging with the happenings or coping with the problems and conflicts and hassles that arise      implies that your own personal safety can be in danger by an uncool person's behavior
      saying that someone is uncool amounts to character assassination among the happeners and one with such a reputation might be ostracized

**underground**   a name many happeners use to describe the tenuously bound subculture its inhabitants and its activities

**up**   most specifically under the influence of one of the psychedelics particularly lsd      more generally to be on a trip and therefore preoccupied and perhaps a little unpredictable but not dangerous in action      others are under some obligation to support and protect the sanctity of someone else's up unless they themselves are being hurt by it

**uptight**   particularly nervous and tense

**where it's at**   the physical or psychological locus or real and significant activity as opposed to sham and ritual

**wig**   your mind

**wig out**   see blow your mind